D1032365

STRATEGY AS RATIONALITY

Strategy as Rationality

Re-directing strategic thought and action

ALAN E. SINGER
Department of Management
University of Canterbury
Christchurch
New Zealand

McK
HD
30.28
.S535
1996

Avebury

Aldershot • Brookfield USA • Hong Kong • Singapore • Sydney

© A. E. Singer 1996

All rights reserved. No part of this publication may be reproduced, stored in a retrieval system, or transmitted in any form or by any means, electronic, mechanical, photocopying, recording or otherwise without the prior permission of the publisher.

Published by
Avebury
Ashgate Publishing Limited
Gower House
Croft Road
Aldershot
Hants GU11 3HR
England

Ashgate Publishing Company
Old Post Road
Brookfield
Vermont 05036
USA

British Library Cataloguing in Publication Data

Singer, Alan E.
    Strategy as Rationality: Re-directing
    Strategic Thought and Action
    I. Title
    128.3

ISBN 1 85972 270 9

Library of Congress Catalog Card Number: 95-83283

Printed and bound by Athenaeum Press, Ltd.,
Gateshead, Tyne & Wear.

Contents

Figures and tables

Acknowledgements

This book and the research upon which it has been based could not have been completed without the support of the Management Department at the University of Canterbury, particularly the outstanding word-processing services of Irene Joseph, with periods of leave hosted by the University of Western Australia and The University of Hawaii at Manoa. There has been much additional encouragement and constructive criticism of the material from the many journal reviewers and their editors. In this regard I would especially like to thank Professor Milan Zeleny (Fordham University) the editor-in-chief of *Human Systems Management*, for his magnificent support.

In addition, thanks are also due to Professor Dan Schendel (Purdue University), editor of the *Strategic Management Journal*; Professor Samuel Eilon (Imperial College, London University) and Professor George Mitchell (London School of Economics & Political Science), past and present editors of *OMEGA*. Also acknowledged are specific contributions from Professor La Rue Hosmer (University of Michigan), Professor Bob Wood (University of Western Australia) Professor Bill Remus (University of Hawaii) and Professor Muhittin Oral (Universite Laval). Their combined leadership, insights, encouragements and accommodations have been vital.

Credits

Chapters 2 & 3
Selected material reprinted from: Alan E. Singer, "Meta-rationality and strategy" *OMEGA*, 19, 2, 1991, pp 101-110. Copyright (1991), with kind permission from Elsevier Science Ltd, The Boulevard, Langford Lane, Kidlington OX5 1GB, United Kingdom.

"Strategy as rationality" *Human Systems Management* 11, 1, 1992 pp 7-21. Copyright (1992) selected material reprinted by permission of the editor.

"Strategy as moral philosophy" *Strategic Management Journal*, 15, 1994, pp 191-213. Copyright (1994) includes selected material reprinted by permission of John Wiley & Sons Ltd.

"Strategic thinking without boundaries" *Systems Practice* 1995 by permission of Plenum Publishing Corporation.

Chapters 4 & 5
Alan E. Singer, "Meta-rationality and strategy" *OMEGA*, 19, 2, 1991 pp101-110. "DCF without forecasts" *OMEGA*, 22, 3 1994. Includes selected material reprinted by permission.

Chapter 6
Alan E. Singer, "Strategy with sunk costs" *Human Systems Management*, 12, 2, 1993. Includes selected material reprinted by permission of the editor.

Chapter 7
Alan E. Singer, "Competitiveness as hyper-strategy" *Human Systems Management* 14, 2, 163-178. Include selected material reprinted by permission of the editor.

Preface

The knowledge that human rationality is itself an active field of inquiry should be a rather sobering thought for those who confidently peddle straightforward remedies to contemporary managerial problems. Yet, so far, the strategic management discipline has merely flirted with a few of the elements of a quite general theory of rationality. Accordingly, this book represents an attempt to develop that flirtation into a much deeper and more formal relationship.

Following the introduction, chapters 2 to 8 of "Strategy as Rationality" contain some of the material that first appeared in several earlier journal articles and conference proceedings (Singer 1991 *et seq*), but in re-arranged form, abridged and developed. These chapters elaborate upon the fundamental theme of an *isomorphism* between a structured rationality-set and a corresponding strategy-set. Hence the title of the book. The main extensions of Strategy-as Rationality deal with (i) the fundamental equivalence of strategic management and business ethics (chapters 2 & 3); (ii) the adaptation of formal models from financial-theory and game-theory (chapters 4, 5 & 7); the problem of strategic decisions involving sunk costs (chapter 6) and, in chapter 7, the necessary re-conceptualizations of competitiveness and competitive strategy. At the same time, some new practical methodologies of strategic analysis are also described in the book. These are: *SCIO, Fake-casting, Ultra-games* and *Meta-Decision-Analysis*.

At a few points throughout the text, mathematical notation has been used (i.e. sets, $\mathbf{R}$, $\mathbf{S}$, and mappings $\mathscr{F}$, ∂, etc.). The meanings are all listed in the Glossary. However, absolutely no mathematical expertise is needed, as the main ideas throughout the book are fully conveyed by the text, with some simple diagrams. Despite the absence of mathematical derivations, there remains, in the author's mind, a loose association between the new frameworks and the formal mathematics of *Category Theory*. The latter branch of algebra features algebraic structures like groups, rings, and integral-domains as its basic elements, but models their inter-relationships. It seems to me that some correspondingly general but similarly formal framework has long been missing from the integrative strategic management discipline. Strategy as Rationality represents but one attempt to fill that theoretical gap.

For practising strategic managers, however, the immediate message of Strategy-as-Rationality is much more straightforward. It may be summarised, quite simply, as follows:

The things you should do as a strategic manager, acting on behalf of any type of strategic entity, are precisely the things that you would do as a balanced and integrated person.

In particular, this means that the rules of business strategy can no longer be set apart from the "business" of social, cultural and moral life. All of these dimensions of human thought and action have important links with the general theory of rationality, hence also strategy. Accordingly, it is hoped that the extended frameworks in this book prove to be of at least some interest not only to management practitioners and strategy experts, but also to researchers across the entire spectrum of the social and managerial sciences, including Economics and Philosophy.

Glossary

A	The generalised strategic-entity. The agent or subject of strategic management theory, when the latter is broadly interpreted. *A* could be an individual, firm, organisation, subsystem, network, alliance, etc. In "Strategy as Rationality" *A* is conceived of as an abstract but *plurally-rational* entity.
$a \in \mathbf{A}$	a is an asset (e.g. a new plant) an element of the set **A**, of suitable assets in an asset-selection decision.
$\partial : \mathbf{M} \Rightarrow \mathbf{R}$	*Decision-function-rationality*. A mapping from the set of models to their implicit or underlying rationalities.
E	The entity-set. The set of possible specific strategic-entities.
$\mathscr{F} : \mathbf{R} \Rightarrow \mathbf{S}$	A mapping from the rationality-set to the strategy set (an *isomorphism*, or structure-preserving map)
J	The Japanese industrial system (as a specific strategic entity).
MDA	Meta-decision-analysis. Deliberation on language categories, forms of rationality and formal models.
$m \in \mathbf{M}$	m is a model, an element of **M**, the set of models.
$\mathbf{M}^{NORM}$	Normative theory. The set of normative models.
$\mathbf{M}^{DESC}$	Descriptive theory. The set of descriptive models.

P^{NORM}	The set of prescriptions flowing from normative theory.
P^{DESC}	The set of prescriptions flowing from descriptive theory (or more accurately, from its local meta-theory).
$\mathcal{P}$	A project, plan, proposal, or strategic option.
$\mathcal{P}^{ALT}$	An alternative to $\mathcal{P}$.
$\mathcal{P}+$	$\mathcal{P}$ continued, after some time t.
$\mathcal{P}-$	$\mathcal{P}$ to-date, before some time t.
$r \in \mathbf{R}$	r is a distinctive form or rationality (e.g. *bounded*). r is an element of the set $\mathbf{R}$, the *plural-rationality-set*.
r^m	A form of rationality implicit in the model m.
$(r_i, r_j) \in \mathbf{R} \times \mathbf{R}$	A meta-rational relationship.
$r \sim s$	r corresponds with s (under the mapping $\mathcal{F}$).
$\mathbf{R}^{EC} \subset \mathbf{R}$	The *economic*-rationality-set, a subset of $\mathbf{R}$.
$\overline{\mathbf{R}}^{EC}$	The complement of $\mathbf{R}$; other forms of rationality.
$\mathbf{R}^{RUM}$	The set of rationalities that are (for some purposes arguably) reducible to *rational utility maximisation (RUM)*.
$\mathbf{R}^{FOW}$	The set of forward-looking forms of rationality.
$\mathbf{R}^{BAK}$	The set of backward-looking forms of rationality
$\mathbf{R}^{BAK*}$	The subset of $\mathbf{R}^{BAK}$ whose elements are not implicit in existing models of strategy with sunk costs.
$(s_k, s_l) \in \mathbf{S} \times \mathbf{S}$	A strategy interface relationship.
$s \in \mathbf{S}$	s is a core concept in strategic management theory, an element of the set $\mathbf{S}$, the *strategy*-set.
SCIO	Specifying canonical issues and options. A technique of inquiry based upon *plural* rationality.
$\mathbf{W}$	The *Weberian* rationalities, i.e.(i) *formal* (ii) *practical* (or action) (iii) *theoretical* (scientific, intensive) (iv) *substantive* (i.e. with respect to values, *wertrationalitat*).
$y \in \mathbf{Y}^{[A]}$	y is a form of synergy amongst the rationalities in the synergy-set $\mathbf{Y}^{[A]}$ of a given entity A.
υ	A mapping of subsets of $\mathbf{R}$ onto synergies.

1. Introduction

In the last quarter of the 13 century A.D., in the shadow of the failure of the Crusades, the author and theologian Ramon Lull had become convinced that comprehensive rational argument might be more effective than military power, for bringing about necessary religious conversions. Accordingly, he created a number of heuristic devices, or decision aids, for helping to convert his Jewish and Muslim contemporaries to Christianity (Gardner, 1958). Understandably, however, Lull's work provoked a deep, violent and lasting controversy. Not only was he stoned to death for his efforts by an angry crowd, but publications attacking and defending him continued to appear more than six hundred years later. Even in quite recent times, there still remain some enthusiastic admirers of the man and his prolific works.

Lull's great art, or *ars magna* involved the identification and classification of multiple attributes of God (e.g. goodness, truthfulness, glory, etc) and some 16 so-called levels-of-nature (e.g. power, justice, blame, ignorance, etc). Each was inscribed onto elaborate circular patterns and careful consideration was then given to *all* the inter-relationships amongst the attributes and the levels. This device generated new arguments to help him influence others' beliefs and thereby facilitate what we might now describe as *ideological transitions*.

A distant echo of Lull's methodologies lives on today, within the corporate towers and teams of the 1990's. The *Ars Magna* has much in common with contemporary management decision aids, such as the 5-forces diagram (Porter, 1980), Graphical Margin-Turnover analyses and the various BCG and PIMS matrices. Like the *ars magna,* these also appeal strongly to the aesthetic sensibilities of members of the power-elite, or the aristocracy, of the day. The *ars magna* is itself generally acknowledged as the origin or precursor of *morphological analysis*, a technique often used now to assist with the product-innovation process (Wills et al, 1972). Lull, however, did not seek to merely influence the occasional strategic decision, rather his mission was nothing less than to bring about fundamental and widespread cultural and ideological change. And it is this aspect that is of special relevance to the framework of "Strategy as Rationality" set out in this book.

An updated version of the *Ars magna* now seems highly appropriate as a way of facilitating more contemporary but equally controversial ideological transitions. Following the enlightenment period of Western civilisation, such an update might simply replace Lull's "attributes of God" with multiple forms of rationality, the rationality-set, whose elements must be placed in relation with one another, using meta-rational arguments. A further, post-capitalist revision of the ars magna might then replace Lull's various "levels of nature" with multiple types of strategic-entity, the entity-set, whose elements are not only individuals, but also teams, virtual-corporates, strategic-alliances, etc. A morphological analysis with these two attribute-dimensions, plural-rationalities and multiple entities, then provides a most useful framework for understanding and advocating another necessary ideological transition: from the self interested and increasingly iron-fisted managerial ideology of property-ownership, with profit-maximisation, towards a far richer ideology of the pragmatic management of multiple human systems.

The rationality-set

In the field of strategic management, or strategy, the role of rationality is often identified with Economic theory, like the contributions from Williamson (1975), Porter (1980, *et seq)* and others (Figure 1.1). However, with few exceptions, the tendency towards formalisation and aggregation in Economic theory has created quite a wide perceived gap between that particular body of theory and recipes for successful business practices (e.g. Rumelt et al, 1991;. Kay, 1991; Grubel and Boland, 1986). It is the major purpose of this book to show that the linkages and inter-relationships between "strategy" and "rationality" do not have to reside entirely within the domain of Economics. They may also be productively and usefully forged in a quite different way.

As Table 1.1. indicates, many distinctive forms of rationality (e.g. *bounded, systemic, selective*, etc.) defined and elaborated upon within the various branches of Economic theory, each themselves, capture simple but rather important prescription for managers. Put differently, there is

2

Table 1.1
Economic-rationalities and strategy-prescriptions

Branch of economic theory	Form(s) of rationality	General prescription for management practice *i.e. Managers should...*
Transaction-cost e.g. WILLIAMSON 1975, TEECE 1982	*bounded, weak*	...take into account the costs of information search and processing (in decisions about strategy and structure)
I/O & Game Theoretic e.g. PORTER 1980, SALONER 1991	*strategic*	...consider the reactions of other entities to your moves and others' moves. Hence take into account reputations, beliefs, signals, etc.
Evolutionary NELSON *et al* 1982	*systemic, adaptive*	...learn from past mistakes. Discover rules in the environment. Utilise experience to continually refine beliefs.
x-efficiency LEIBENSTEIN 1976	*selective, ratchet*	...seek motivational devices that improve capabilities and develop the full potential of the firm. Allow for organisational inertia, or *status-quo* bias.
Behavioral SCHWENK 1984, HOGARTH *et al* 1981	*cognitive, quasi*	...take into account systematic biases, heuristic use, costs of search and processing for self (i.e. *meta*-cognition) and for others. Avoid waste.

a well-defined set of *economic*-rationalities that, by themselves, inform strategic management quite directly, without invoking the details of any aggregate-level economic theory.

To the extent that the *economic*-rationality-set informs strategy in the way indicated in Table 1, it must now also be asked whether or not other forms of rationality might do the same. In answering this question in the affirmative, this book, like the related journal articles (Singer 1991 *et seq*) draws upon an emerging general theory of rational and ethical behaviour, that involves the identification and classification of multiple or *plural* behavioral prescriptions, together with partial accounts of their inter-relationships, or *meta*-relations. In many ways, the theory set out in the book is evocative of earlier work by the American *Pragmatists* (Charles Pierce, James Dewey and William James). Writing a century after Adam Smith first laid down the conceptual foundation of modern Economics, these Pragmatists, like the present book, sought to respond to the changing relationships between action, belief and knowledge that were being brought about by the scientific and technological advances of the time.

Plural-rationality concepts have been around for some time, often implicit, within the strategic management and planning disciplines. For example, some have commented on what they see as "uncanny" parallels between *cognitive* dimensions of rationality and modern planning and forecasting concepts, whilst others have noted close parallels between administrative problems and questions of ethics and values (*evaluative* or *ends*-rationality). However, many developments in the general theory of rationality that have taken place during the 1980s and beyond, have largely been ignored in strategic management theory and research. Thus, to paraphrase Burrell (1989), strategic management theory has, until quite recently, suffered from "an absent centre", at least with respect to its prescriptive dimensions.

It has often been noted before (e.g. Bryman, 1984) that an exclusion of rationality concepts from management theory seems premature, so long as rationality itself remains an active field of enquiry. The book develops this theme to its ultimate conclusion by arguing that the categories of meaning associated with individual "rationality" and collective "strategy" are, in fact, the same. The significance of this, in turn, lies in its implications for what strategic level managers should do, when they act on behalf of any strategic entity (firm, team, virtual corporation, alliance, etc.) Accordingly, in chapter 2 of the book, the correspondences mentioned in Table 1.1., between strategy and rationality (i.e. the strategy ~ rationality relation) are elaborated and extended. A structure-preserving mapping, or *isomorphism* is made explicit, thereby forging a direct link between *plural*-rationality concepts (formally, a rationality-set, **R**) and core concepts of strategic management (the strategy-set, **S**).

4

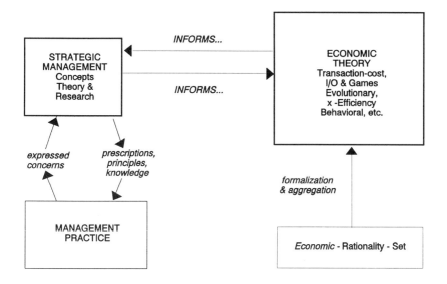

Figure 1.1 Strategy and economic rationality

Strategic entities

When we talk about "strategic management" *who* or *what* is being managed? The advent of the boundary-less "organisation" and the global post-industrial society has repeatedly raised the question of the nature and identity of the unit of analysis in strategic management, the strategic-entity, without ever providing a clear and satisfying answer. Indeed, as various forms of strategic alliance have become ever more commonplace, doubts have been openly voiced about those concepts of "Strategy" that implicitly assume business-as-usual (e.g. Baccaracco, 1992). In short, the question of whose strategy is being managed and whose "competitive advantage" is being sought by today's managers and policy makers, is being asked more and more often. Many practitioners' discussions and academics' theories of strategy and policy decisions now reveal a disturbing ambiguity concerning the nature, identity and boundary of the decision-making agent, the unit of analysis, or the strategic entity that owns or implements strategies and policies. More specifically, many are now asking *who* or *what* is:

> *DECIDING* in theories of decision-making (e.g. Grinyer, 1992, Boland *et al* 1994).
> *BEING RATIONAL* in economic and other models (e.g.

5

Schoemaker, 1993, Singer, 1992).
BEING MORAL in ethical theory and business-ethics (e.g. Singer, 1994a, Werhane, 1983).
COMPETING against (and co-operating with) whom (e.g. Singer & Brodie 1990, Nielsen, 1988, Singer, 1993b).
TRUSTING whom, for example, in the international arena (e.g. Parke, 1993).

These and other similar questions might be regarded by some as research issues in their own right, by others as sources of tolerable ambiguity, or else simply as roadblocks in the path of inquiry (e.g. Levi, 1986).

Morphology

With the latter pragmatic viewpoint one could simply bypass this roadblock, in order to explore new possibilities and interpretations of contemporary managerial activity. Thus, by combining plural rationalities with multiple strategic entities together into another, higher level matrix...a morphological space...one is launched into an exploration of the *terra incognita* of the managerial and policy sciences themselves, the undiscovered country for strategic management theory.

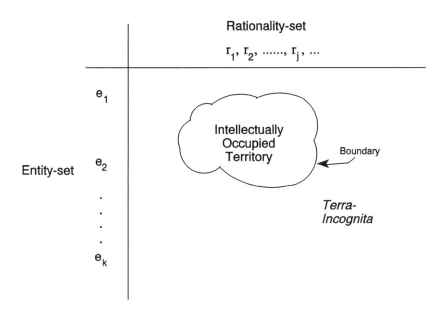

Figure 1.2 A morphological analysis

6

For each of the above questions about types of entity, the possible answers must now include:

Trans-national-institution (e.g. MNC), regional-bloc, nation-state, community, industry, strategic -group; alliance or consortium, network, flex-firm, team, traditional firm, or organisation, business-unit or segment, division, department, group, dominant-coalition, CEO, individual, household, psychological-self, cognitive-system, brain, etc.

Collectively, these entities may be regarded as comprising an entity-set, **E**, a dimension in the morphological space of Figure 1.2. The sets **R** (plural rationality) and **E** (multiple entity types) can then be conceived of as a pair of axes in the morphological space, **R** x **E**. Exploration of the neighbourhoods of the intellectually-occupied-territory (ie. conventional theory) then becomes suggestive of the novel possibilities for strategic analysis discussed throughout this book.

Strategy as rationality

First steps have already been taken, for example, in re-conceptualising competitiveness (Oral et al, 1989, Singer, 1993b), in analysing strategy with sunk-costs (Singer 1993c) and in business-ethics (Singer, 1984 & 1994a, Singer & van der Walt, 1987). More generally, the morphological analysis reveals the necessity for (i) *meta*-decision analysis in strategy and policy decisions, and (ii) suitable transitional methodologies, for redirecting strategic thinking. These are also to be elaborated in subsequent chapters.

In "Strategy as Rationality", the conceptual framework set out in the following chapter, the strategic-entity *A* is identified as a *plurally* rational agent (i.e. the subject of general theories of rationality). The processes and rationales that mediate strategic behaviour are, at the same time, seen as completely transcending the distinction between types of agent. That is, they apply to any or all of the elements of the entity-set. The behaviour of a generalised strategic entity *A* is thus seen as conforming at various times to all of the distinctive forms of rationality, which are assumed to *co-exist* as behavioral properties of the entity. This viewpoint, that all strategic entities should be conceived of as *plurally* rational agents and managed accordingly is far easier to defend and much richer in its implications than the main alternative viewpoint that sees such entities as *utility maximisers*, or simply as *bounded* within their own self-interested strategic thinking.

Ethics

According to Georges Kervern of the Union Des Assurances in Paris (1991), an integration of corporate strategy with ethics is potentially *"une therapeutic - la moins violente possible - des maladies de la societe"*. Akio Morita, chairman of Sony, has expressed the view that Japanese corporations must start to "think differently... treating employees more humanely whilst contributing more to the community and environmental protection". The new framework of strategy as rationality places all such imperatives in a coherent context. If "strategy", like "rationality", broadly conceived, is concerned with problems of action, decision and behaviour set in socio-economic contexts, then so too is the subject of Ethics, or Moral-Philosophy. This leads directly to the conclusion, set out chapter three, that strategic management and business ethics are the same subject. The organisation or strategic entity simply becomes re-cast as a moral-agent. Normative ethical theory is thus linked directly to prescription in strategic management.

According to some economic and political theories, this notion of "Business Ethics", implied in this equation of strategy with ethics, is naive and mistaken, unless it is intended as a mere public-relations or marketing *ploy* (e.g. Friedman, 1970). However, others have pointed to quite specific improvements in society, culture and economy that could be expected to flow from corporate motivations that genuinely transcend the rationality of *utility maximisation,* which is manifest in profit maximisation goals, with profit-oriented incentive structures. The framework of Strategy as Moral Philosophy, described in chapter three, simply offers a corresponding justification for the moral dimension, within a theory of strategic management.

Models

In the fourth chapter of the book, on "reconciliations", the question of conflicting model-based strategy prescriptions, particularly financial versus strategic analysis, is considered. Such conflicts have been considered paradoxical (e.g. Bowman, 1980) or as a technical challenge. Yet, when they occur in practice, they can simply serve to draw attention to the fallibility of any particular formal model, theory, or *Weltanschauung*. Model-based strategy prescriptions may be analysed at three levels: at the first level are the various alternative decision-models and techniques themselves, together with questions about their inter-relationships. At the second level is the plural rationality of the strategic entity. Forms of rationality can be placed in correspondence with the various models and strategic principles, using the concept of a mapping, decision-function-rationality, originally due to Morecroft (1983). At the third level are the various inter-relationships between the multiple forms of rationality, the meta-rational arguments.

Chapter five then pursues a complementary path towards reconciling strategic analysis with model-based financial analysis of investment proposals. The difficulties experienced by managers trying to incorporate strategic issues into cashflow forecasts, for conventional financial analysis, are explained here with reference to the impossibility of forecasting reliably in volatile and chaotic environments. Given the very widespread current use of forecast based models like net-present-value, any proposal to totally abandon these models in favour of forecast-free or *plurally* rational alternatives (a *meta*-modelling decision) is likely to encounter strong resistance. Accordingly, it is proposed that traditional methodologies like NPV could be retained for some time, but adapted by treating the models as devices for evoking knowledge from memory. This is in line with the perspective on strategic entities as knowledge systems.

The proposed adaptations of DCF point once more to the wider question of how, in practical terms, to facilitate and implement transitions between old and new methodologies and ideologies. To date, this has been relatively neglected, as an area of meta-theory. With the concept of decision-function-rationality in place, the process of transition from DCF methodology towards alternative problem structuring methods becomes re-cast as a transition between rationalities. Rather similar ideas were first documented by Ramon Lull...over 700 years ago.

Re-considerations

Chapter six tackles the vexed problem of sunk costs in strategic and financial re-appraisals of capital projects. Within the framework of "Strategy as Rationality" this widely studied problem is seen to be equivalent (*isomorphic*) to that confronting a plurally-rational individual who cannot be certain about the future but is re-considering a partially-implemented personal plan. A generic sunk-cost problem is defined involving a *plurally*-rational agent, or strategic entity, and a project, plan, program, or strategy that is being re-considered.

On the face of it there are already several types of theory that seem directly relevant to the sunk cost problem, thus stated. These include normative, descriptive and hybrid theories. The prescriptions for

9

managers that flow from the existing theories, with their respective meta-theoretic commentaries, may be usefully summarised as follows: (i) enrich the content of the strategic decision, (ii) improve the process, and (iii) develop new theory. "Strategy as Rationality" falls within the latter category, i.e. new theory. Specifically, it is possible to extend the analysis of strategy with sunk costs by focusing more closely upon the *backward-looking* rationalities, a subset of the plural rationalities. This, in turn, yields several questions that managers should reflect upon.

Competition

The orientation towards specific applications is then continued, with a particular focus upon competition, competitor analysis and "competitiveness". The latter is only rarely defined in a way that carries coherent strategic implications. In practice, missions of "achieving competitiveness" often translate into improving productivity by implementing strategies of business process re-engineering, cost-reduction, downsizing, re-sourcing and automation. In many cases these lead to wage reductions and fewer jobs (at least when compared to the *status quo ante*) both within and beyond the boundaries of the "re-engineered" strategic entity. The problem is that when many entities do this, the result is social inequity and potential instability.

At the core of the ethics and politics of competitiveness lie at least two ambiguities. The first concerns the definition and scope of the "competitive" strategic entity (i.e. *Who* or *what* is being "competitive" against *whom*?) and the second concerns the distinction between winning, or victory, *versus* success, or realisation-of-potential. These two ambiguities are closely related, as "achieving competitiveness" could simply be taken to mean overcoming limitations within the strategic entity, rather than necessarily outperforming or defeating other entities. With the framework of "strategy as rationality" in place, the concept of the *hyper*-rationality of industrial systems, due to Ritzer & Le Moyne (1991), may be extended and re-interpreted, to yield a new conception of the *hyper*-strategy of all strategic entities. The latter involves the strategic entity A and the set R of the *plural*-rationalities, but also synergies between the forms of rationality. Two examples are: (i) In the Japanese industrial system, the "bottom-up" practical rationality is reinforced by the ethic of "groupism" (i.e. synergy between *practical & substantive* Weberian forms), and (ii) In IBM corporation, in the 1960's financial successes were used to reinforce a sense of identity (i.e. synergy between the *utility maximisation* implicit in corporate financial objectives & the *expressive* forms of rationality that are implicit in the search for a collective identity).

Conclusion

The various threads of strategy as rationality are drawn together in the concluding chapter. The coverage of ethics, histories, competition and model-use, taken together, indicate that it is not only strategic entities that are reshaping their boundaries, but it is also strategic thinking that is expanding beyond its more traditional constraints. Boundaryless strategic thinking must spans multiple rationalities, diverse categories of meaning, new language and alternative models.

This type of thinking, or at least the transition towards it, can be facilitated with the SCIO technique of inquiry based upon plural rationality (chapter 3), but also by using the other techniques outlined in chapters 5, 7 and 8. *Meta*-decision-analysis (chapter 8) attempts to help strategic managers who are acting on behalf of any type of strategic entity, to choose rationalities, formal models and especially language, more carefully. For any strategic entity and for any strategic decision, these three meta-decisions (rationalities, categories, models) must be dealt with concurrently, as a crucial and integral part of the strategy process. By redirecting strategic thought in this way, strategic entities should become much more capable of producing not only their marketed outputs, but also their future selves. They will become *autopoeitic...* remaking themselves...by remaking their speech (cf. Rorty, 1982) and their understandings.

2. Strategy as rationality

Multiple but distinctive forms of rationality have been defined and employed in studies of decision making and behaviour across the entire spectrum of the social and economic sciences (e.g. Binmore, 1987, Cherniak, 1986, Elster, 1979 *et seq*, March, 1978, Sen, 1977, Simon, 1987, Hargreaves-Heap, 1989, to mention a few). Figure 2.1 and Table 2.1 present a taxonomy of many of these forms. They also illustrate the idea of a general theory of rationality, an interwoven fabric (cf. Rescher, 1988) that involves not only the identification of multiple forms of rationality, elements of the rationality-set **R**, but also the specification or construction of:

(i)   meta-rational criteria for classifying the r ϵ **R** (e.g. *calculated vs. systemic; belief, means, ends-oriented, backward-looking* etc.)

(ii)   evaluative meta-rational criteria for the r ϵ **R** (e.g. *universalizable, global, self-supporting*, etc.) and

(iii)   meta-rational arguments or relationships in **R** x **R** and their power-sets, that place elements and subsets of **R** in relation to each other (e.g. *RUM*-capture, belief-ends relations, etc.)

The subject of meta-rationality has also featured in many different disciplines (e.g. Jungerman, 1983, Hamlin, 1986, Martinelli, 1991, Van Gigch, 1991). Within the general theory of rationality, it is helpful to first distinguish calculated versus *systemic* forms of means-rationality, then other "*means*-rationalities", "*belief*-rationalities" and "*ends*-rationalities" (cf. Hamlin, 1986). At the same time, it is also possible to identify some quite direct linkages to topics of recognised importance within strategic management theory and practice, or "strategy".

First, *calculated versus systemic* forms may be distinguished (March, 1978). Calculated rationality embraces the entire process of goal-setting, belief-verification and discovery of suitable means for achievement of those goals. By contrast, systemic forms like *selective* rationality are backward-looking in the sense that their definition involves some reference to historical contexts. Under a criterion of selective rationality, a decision to act is deemed rational if similar acts in similar circumstances have, in the past, enabled survival and development of the decision-making agent. Similarly, *posterior* rationality refers to the pursuit of goals that have themselves emerged from past experiences; whilst *adaptive* rationality refers to the use of decision-making rules derived in that way.

Corresponding to this, a strategic decision by an organisation, reflecting a tradition of internal development (e.g. in the face of an acquisition proposal having high forecast profitability) could be adaptively rational, even if not in the calculated sense. Conflicts surrounding such strategic decisions might then be understood in terms of the *meta*-rational relationships between these forms of rationality (refer to chapter 4).

Economic theory has traditionally been concerned with the *means*-rationality of the decision-making agent (model-user or problem-owner) and particularly with the *substantive* forms that refer to outcomes. These may be distinguished from *procedural* forms involving rule-governed processes in decision making. An emphasis on process rather than outcome also distinguishes *imperfect* from *perfect* forms. The latter assume total knowledge of the relevant environment (omniscience) and outcomes, whilst imperfect forms emphasise procedures that help overcome the decision maker's recognised limitations.

Bounded rationality is one particularly richly-described form of imperfect rationality. It has been widely interpreted (Schwenk, 1984, Simon, 1987) in terms of individual cognitive processes (limited attention, cognitive heuristics, satisfying, etc.) and their organisational counterparts (costs of information, problem identification, procedural rules, acceptability criteria, etc.) Many strategy techniques that assist the decision maker in structuring limited relevant knowledge implicitly assume bounded rationality, or some other *imperfect* form.

Weakness-of-will is another imperfect form (Hamlin, 1986) that accommodates the possible instability of the agent's goals over time, so that binding precommitments become rational, as in the mythical

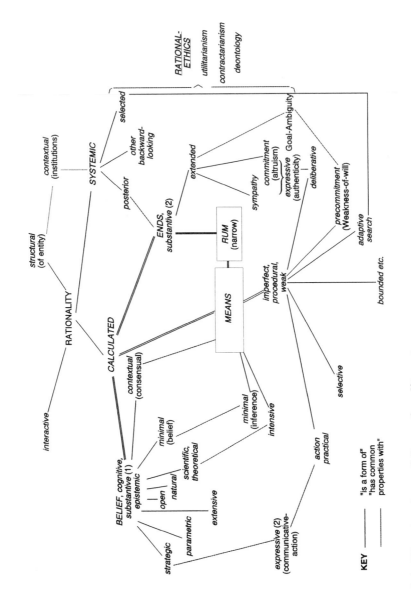

Figure 2.1 The structure of the rationality-set

14

behaviour of Ulysses' who deliberately bound himself to his ship's mast (Elster, 1979). With this concept of rationality, a strategic investment could be deemed rational simply if it were considered to constrain future possible changes of goal.

In other cases of decisional conflict and doubt, there might be straightforward disagreements over the relevant facts. Such disagreements are the focus of *belief*-rationalities. Evidence shows that contrasting beliefs may often be characterised in terms of *parametric* versus *strategic* forms of rationality (Einhorn et al, 1982, Elster, 1979). The former entails non-recognition of environmental (e.g. stakeholder) responsiveness, or else some misperception of the controllability of the environment (e.g. Langer, 1975). In a planning context, such misperceptions sometimes occur concerning factors like the ability to influence legislation, or the degree of causality entailed by known statistical relationships, like the ROI ~ market share link.

The overlooking of important but available information is another aspect or dimension of belief-rationality most relevant to strategic decisions. The activation of (at least some) relevant beliefs, or knowledge, has been identified as a requirement for *minimal* rationality (Cherniak, 1986). Therefore, this particular form of rationality is implicit in decision-making techniques that involve checklists of relevant factors, assumptions-surfacing and testing (Mason et al, 1981), or "brainstorming", in the strategy process.

Finally, concerning the definition of rational goals or *ends*, the distinction between self-interested rational-*egoism* versus *extended* forms of rationality (i.e. others' interests) and the further distinction between rational-*sympathy* and rational-*commitments*, is also most relevant to problems of strategy. "Sympathy" (e.g. Sen, 1977) is where concern for others directly effects one's own welfare, as mirrored in the stakeholder approach to strategic management. Commitments, by contrast, can involve the concept of counterpreferential choices where utility is deliberately sacrificed for other purposes (after allowing for psychological empathy). In the following section, several other elements of the rationality-set are described and their linkage with strategy is made much more explicit.

Isomorphism

The correspondences between rationality concepts and strategy concepts that were suggested above can be extended and made much more explicit by comparing Figure 2.1 (above) with Figure 2.2. The multiple forms of rationality, considered collectively, may be thought of as comprising a structured set, **R**. In the remainder of the book, the term *plural* rationality (originally due to Grauer et al, 1984) is used to refer to this entire rationality-set, as a whole. The elements of **R** are listed in Tables 2.1-2.7, together with their *images* in **S**. Using the symbol " ~ " to refer to correspondence or relationship, the organisation of these tables could be described as follows:

1. *Belief*-rationalities ~ managerial-perspectives and expectations;
2. *Means* -rationalities ~ strategic decision processes;
3. *Action* rationalities ~ logical incrementalism;
4. *Backward-looking* rationalities ~ historical processes;
5. *Interactive* rationality ~ predicting or diagnosing strategy.
6. *Ends* -rationalities ~ corporate objectives and missions;
7. Rational-*morality* ~ managerial ethics.

The tables show how the rationality set **R** may be placed in a one-to-one correspondence with a strategy-set **S**, whose elements include: the stakeholder approach, capability-development, identity-preservation, assumptions surfacing and testing, etc. Moreover, the many inter-relationships within the strategy-set **S** (i.e. relationships in **S** x **S**, or strategy-interfaces) which are frequently the subject of direct empirical investigation in strategy research, are, at the same time, mapped onto the various *meta*-rational relationships (in **R** x **R**). For example, just as STAKEHOLDERS-AS-CONSTRAINTS (Ansoff, 1965) --*is a form of* -- organisational goal-structure, so, in a corresponding sense, RATIONAL-SYMPATHY (Sen, 1977) --*is a form of*-- ends-rationality. More specifically, a relational structure may now be implanted in **R** (and hence in **S**) using two types of *meta*-rational relation:

(i)   "r_i is a form of r_j". For example, sympathy ...*is a form of...* extended-ends-rationality.

(ii)   "r_k *has significant common properties with* r_l", for example, expressive rationality (which concerns communicative action like signalling)...*has significant common properties with*...Elster's (1986) strategic-belief rationality (which is concerned with game-theoretic interdependencies).

16

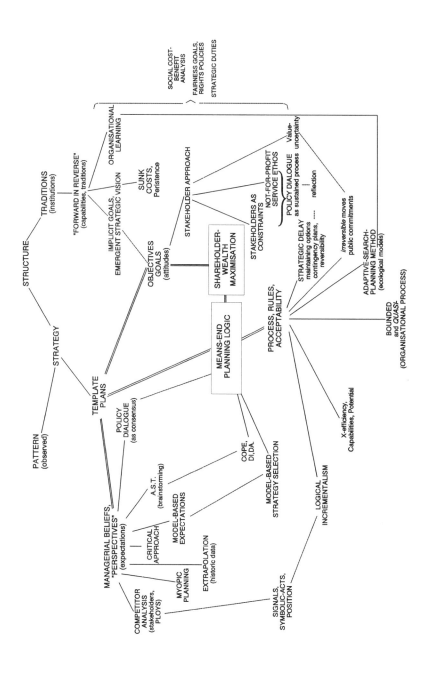

Figure 2.2 The structure of the strategy-set

17

The relational structure in **S** is similar, and is preserved (or, in some cases implanted) by assuming that the one-to-one correspondence between **R** and **S** is a structure-preserving mapping, or *isomorphism* (Figure 2.3.). In that case, corresponding to (i) & (ii) in **R**, we have relationships between the *images* (i)* and (ii)*, as follows:

(i)* Stakeholders-as-constraints (Ansoff, 1965)...*is a form of* ...organisational goal system.

(ii)* Positioning is an ingredient of organisational strategy (e.g. Mintzberg, 1987). This strategy-concept ..*has significant common properties with*...signalling behaviour.

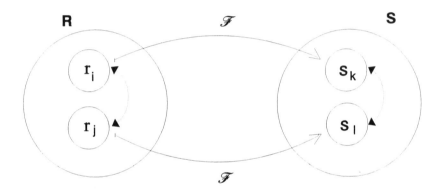

Figure 2.3   Isomorphism between R and S

The pattern of reasoning illustrated by these two examples may be made *quasi*-formal. Let (r_i, r_j) be any pairwise relationship in **R** , that is a *meta*-rational relationship like those described above. The mapping:

$\Im$: **R** $\Rightarrow$ **S** gives:

$\Im (r_i) = s_k$ and $\Im (r_j) = s_l$ for some k, l.

Then, for all i, j, we have:

$\Im \times \Im (r_i, r_j) = [\Im (r_i), \Im (r_j)] = (s_k, s_l)$, for some k, l.

18

The latter pairwise relationship, in **S**, is an interface relationship between a pair of strategy concepts. Expressed in words, "all forms of rationality have their counterpart strategy concepts, whilst the strategy interface concepts reflect the *meta*-rational relationships". That is, $\mathfrak{I}$ is an isomorphism, or structure preserving map that identifies **R** and **S** as essentially the same thing.

Correspondents

Of the many **R** ~ **S** correspondences, the following few are singled out as perhaps especially noteworthy. First, Mintzberg's (1987) "5 P's of Strategy" each correspond to distinctive forms of rationality, as follows: (i) PLANS ~ *calculated* rationality, (calculation of consequences) (ii) PERSPECTIVES ~ *substantive*-belief rationalities (core mental constructs, attitudes) , (ii) PLOYS ~ *strategic* rationality (gaming), (iv) POSITION ~ *expressive* rationality (communicative action, signalling) (v) PATTERN ~ *interactive* rationality ("in the eye of the beholder"). In addition, (vi) LOGICAL INCREMENTALISM in planning ~ "*praxis*" or *action*-rationality, (vii) The use of EXTRAPOLATORY FORECASTS in planning ~ *extensive* belief-rationality in decision-making, (viii) DIALECTICAL INQUIRY methodology ~ *minimal*-rationality, (ix) INTENDED *versus* REALISED strategy ~ *excess-of-will* in rational choice. These correspondences, with many others, are set out in Tables 2.1-2.7.

These correspondences show how the language and concepts of strategic management very closely parallel those of the *plural* rationalities. "Strategy" and "Rationality" are, extensionally, all but equivalent, sharing almost all of their salient features. An **R** ~ **S** isomorphism specified in this way effectively demonstrates that the concepts of strategic-management and *plural*-rationality are co-extensive, meaning that the language and underlying concepts parallel one another. Thus, it not only makes sense to view "Strategy as Rationality", as is done throughout this book, but it also make sense to assert that "strategy *is* rationality". Indeed, what else could it be? What else should it be?

This equivalence, or sameness is no coincidence. It may explained by the simple observation that both sets of concepts (**R** and **S**) have been shaped by those attempting to grapple with quite universal problems of action, decision and behaviour, set in *socio*-economic contexts. Accordingly, one could now say quite categorically that there is a well-developed prescriptive theory of strategic management...it is nothing other than the general theory of rationality.

Table 2.1
Belief rationalities and managerial perspectives

Strategy concept	Form of rationality	References
PERSPECTIVES expectations	*belief, cognitive (substantive, epistemic)*	SIMON (1987) MINTZBERG (1987)
COMPETITOR-ANALYSIS ploys	*strategic*	ELSTER (1979) BINMORE (1987) PORTER (1980)
MYOPIC PLANS	*parametric*	ELSTER (1979) ARGENTI (1980)
EXTRAPOLATION historic data	*extensive*	WALLISER (1989) MAKRIDAKIS (1988)
MODEL-BASED EXPECTATIONS	*scientific, intensive*	WALLISER (1989) FISCHOFF & GOITEN (1984)
COMPLETE FORESIGHT	*perfect (omniscient, strong)*	SIMON (1987) WALLISER (1989)
ASSUMPTIONS-SURFACING & TESTING (& brainstorming)	*minimal-belief*	CHERNIAK (1986) MASON & MITROFF (1981)
ex post strategic REVIEWS	*open natural*	POPPER (1989) HILEY (1979) KITCHENER *et al* (1981)

Table 2.2

Means rationalities and strategic decision processes

MEANS-ENDS PLANNING LOGIC	*instrumental (zweickrationalitat)*	ARGENTI (1980) WEBER (1947)
MAXIMIZATION & OPTIMIZATION	*perfect strong*	SIMON (1987)

MODEL-BASED STRATEGY-SELECTION	*intensive*	WALLISER (1989) ORAL (1986)
PROCESSES, RULES, ACCEPTABILITY	*imperfect procedural weak*	HAMLIN (1986) SIMON (1987)
BOUNDED and *QUASI*-RAT (organisation)	*bounded, quasi*	SIMON (1987) THALER (1985) HOGARTH & MAKRIDAKIS (1981)
ADAPTIVE-SEARCH PLANNING METHOD experiential-learning	*adaptive*	ANSOFF (1987) MARCH 1978)
DI-DA, COPE etc.	*minimal-inference*	CHERNIAK (1986) MASON & MITROFF (1981)
PROMISES, IRREVERSIBLE moves	*pre-commitment, weakness-of-will*	ELSTER (1979) THALER (1981) MARCH (1978)
DELIBERATE vs EMERGENT STRAT.	*excess-of will*	ELSTER (1989) MINTZBERG *et al* (1985)
STRATEGIC DELAY flexibility options-maintenance	*postponement*	AAKER & MASCERENHAS (1984) RAWLS (1972)
X-efficiency CAPABILITIES, Potential	*selective*	LEIBENSTEIN (1976)
POLICY DIALOGUE, PROBLEM-STRUCTURING	*contextual, consensual*	HABERMAS (1981) ROSSOUW (1994)

Table 2.3

Action rationalities and logical incrementalism

LOGICAL INCREMENTALISM	*action-rat., practical-rat.*	WEBER (1947) BRUNSSON (1982) GLADSTEIN *et al* (1985)
SIGNALS, SYMBOLIC ACTS, (Position)	*expressive (2) communicative acts*	HARGREAVES-HEAP (1988) MINTZBERG (1987)

Table 2.4

Backward looking rationalities and historical processes

FORWARD-IN-REVERSE planning logic	*systemic*	MARCH (1978) HAYES (1985)
EMERGENT VISION implicit goals	*posterior*	MARCH (1978) HAYES (1985)
ORGANISATIONAL-TRADITIONS (stability, co-ordination)	*contextual*	WHITE (1988) HABERMAS (1981) MARCH (1978)
STRATEGIC PERSISTENCE (completion of plans)	*constrained resolute*	SLOTE (1989) McLENNEN (1990) SCHWENIC *et al* (1989)
SURVIVAL, ecological-models	*selected (by environment)*	HANNAN & FREEMAN 1980 BETTON & DESS (1985)
STATUS-QUO bias	*retrospective, ratchet (selective)*	STAW (1980) LEIBENSTEIN (1976)

Table 2.5

Interactive rationality and diagnosing strategy

PATTERN emergent	*interactive observer*	MINTZBERG 1987 ACKOFF 1983

Table 2.6

Ends rationalities and corporate missions

OBJECTIVES, GOALS	*value, substantive, (wertrationalitat)*	HAMLIN (1986) WEBER (1947) SIMON (1964)
SHAREHOLDER-WEALTH with mgt. incentives	*self-interest egoism*	RAND (1964) SEN (1977) HALEY & SCHALL (1979)

22

STAKEHOLDER APPROACH	*extended*	SIMON (1964) SEN (1977) FREEMAN (1984)
STAKEHOLDERS AS CONSTRAINTS	*sympathy, interdependent*	SEN (1977) ETZIONI (1986) ANSOFF (1988)
NOT-FOR PROFIT SERVICE ETHOS	*commitment, (altruism)*	SEN (1977) FREEMAN (1984)
Value-uncertainty in planning	*goal ambiguity in rational choice*	MARCH (1978) FRIEND & HICKLING (1987)
formulating objectives (process)	*deliberative, reflective*	RAWLS (1972) QUINN (1977)
POLICY DIALOGUE As autonomous process, *Ringi*	*expressive (1), concern for autonomy*	HARGREAVES-HEAP (1989) PUCIK & HATVANI (1983)

Rational-agency

The existence of isomorphism implies that the identities and natures of the rational-agents, or the strategic-entities, become the most salient differentiating factors for "strategy" and "rationality", conceived of as interdisciplinary fields of inquiry. For the rationality concepts, in **R**, the agent is normally an individual, a thinking, choosing and acting human-being. Yet even this assumption, that rationality inheres in individuals, has started to come under much closer scrutiny, both in theory (e.g. Cudd, 1993) and in applications (e.g. Grinyer, 1992).

It has often been asked whether theories of individual rationality also apply to firms organisations, or other collectivities (e.g., Allison, 1971, Bryman, 1984, Levi, 1986). Many organisational theorists and philosophers have answered this question in the negative, describing the idea as profoundly misleading, even irrational, (e.g., Brunsson, 1982, Pennings, 1985, Elster, 1986). Yet, despite this rejection, notions of collective rational agency have managed to occupy a most distinguished place in the general history of socio-economic ideas. In Plato's *Republic,* for example, the individual was often used as a metaphor for the nation or state, whereas Hobbes used the term "*sovereign*" to refer both to individuals and to parliament. Later still, neo-classical economists treated individuals, households and firms homogeneously, as abstract units of analysis in economic models.

Technical objections to the notion of corporate or collective rational agency have all focused on the hypothetical *rational utility maximiser* of neo-classical economics. Accordingly re-interpretations of "rationality" could comprise a most useful generic defence of the concept of the rational-agency of collectivities. Put differently, the main anti-agency roadblocks may simply be sidestepped, by invoking *plural* rationality concepts. The objections, or "roadblocks" have been built upon considerations such as informational and cognitive limitations, Arrow's social-choice theorem, elements of General Systems Theory and the political-process perspectives on strategic management and decision making. However, with the newer generic defences in place (refer to Appendix 1) the concept of rational-agency in strategic management thinking and research re-emerges in very good shape. In fact, like the mythical *Hydra* of ancient Greece, it has returned with multiple heads in place of just one or two.

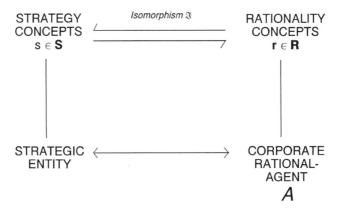

Figure 2.4 Strategy and rational - agency

Strategic mysteries

The framework of strategy as rationality may be used to shed some new light on mysteries of strategy, by re-casting them as equivalent problems of rationality. Just as Economics has often been used to inform strategy (as depicted in Figure 1.1 of the introduction), strategy is potentially also informed by the general theory of rationality (Figure 2.5). And *vice-versa*: empirical strategy research undoubtedly contributes to the continuing evolution of the general theory of rationality.

Amongst the many examples of how *plural* rationality informs strategy are: the optimal strategy problem, expressive strategies, strategic timing, as follows.

i) *Optimal-strategy* The "optimal rationality problem" (Marsh, 1978) concerns ways of balancing calculated forms against rule-based forms (*selective, procedural*, etc). The weak point, or Achilles-heel of calculated forms is the profound non-forecastability of complex social systems (discussed further in chapter 5) which make many outcomes impossible to quantify. On the other hand, the weakness of rule-based forms is found in the limited amount of experience that is summarised by the rules, together with the problem of assessing the degree of similarity between past and current contexts. Strategic-level managers sometimes confront a corresponding "optimal-strategy problem" of balancing their organisational traditions and conservative policy principles against forward-looking or forecast-based strategic or financial analysis.

Another expression of the optimal-strategy problem is found in the rather mysterious "forward-in-reverse planning logic", prescribed a seminal article by Hayes (1985) on corporate strategy. In that article, managers were advised to delay goal-setting on behalf of the strategic entity, until its capabilities have become more fully developed and until a strategy has emerged. Put differently, "means first, goals later (if at all)". This directly violates the more conventional business goal-setting philosophies that require prior articulation of strategic missions and the like (i.e. '*if you don't know where your going…*'). With "strategy-as rationality" in place, the relationship (in **S** x **S**) between these opposing "planning logics" may be more fully understood in terms of general *meta*-rational arguments (in **R** x **R**). For example, goals are often articulated in order to satisfy the psychological needs of influential outsiders, rather than for internal consumption. These points are elaborated in subsequent chapters.

ii) *Non-instrumental, expressive strategies* Corporate investment decisions can sometimes turn on considerations of the autonomy and identity of the entity. For example, entrepreneurial projects such as the

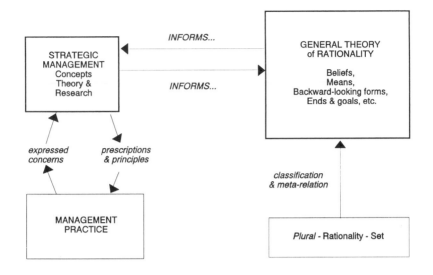

Figure 2.5 Strategy and the general theory of rationality

Federal Express "Zapmail" project, the Hughes Aircraft Corp. "Spruce Goose" and the Anglo-French Concorde SST, were not obviously driven by calculations of anticipated profits. Such calculations, when done, proved to be highly unreliable, since they were exploring the unknown. These major strategic investments could, however, be much more readily understood in terms of *expressive* rationality (e.g., Hargreaves-Heap, 1989). They were symbols of (corporate) capability, or steps in a (collective) search for self-realisation and positive freedom. A *meta*-rational argument now tells us that such strategies absolutely defy attempts at conventional risk-return analysis: expressively-rational actions cannot be reduced to calculated forms of rationality, since the former places intrinsic value on experimentation with preferences or goals, rather than taking these as given (Hargreaves-Heap, 1989).

iii) *Strategic Timing* The concept of "postponement" has been the focus of several economic strategy models (Pindyck, 1991). These models implicity assume *utility maximisation* (discussed further in chapter three) However, other forms of rationality, particularly *precommitment* are also quite relevant to problems of corporate strategic timing. *Postponement* vs. *precommitment* is, in fact, one of the many paradoxes of rationality that is recognized in the general theory. Postponement calls for delay, to obtain further information, but precommitment, as a form of rationality, prescribes immediate action before current goals change. Where both types of uncertainty co-exist, conflicting prescriptions can result. Since pre-emption cannot be reduced to postponement (a *meta*-rational argument) the timing of strategic moves remains as a more fundamental mystery of strategy.

In addition, to optimal and expressive strategies and the mysteries of timing, several other similar developments, flowing from "rationality" to "strategy", are elaborated in subsequent chapters of the book. These include the rationality ~ ethics linkages, with strategic sympathy and commitments (chapter 3), strategy with sunk-costs (chapter 6), as well as "competitiveness as hyper-strategy" (chapter 7).

Strategy also informs rationality

Strategy research involving organisations could also contribute to the solution of longstanding philosophical problems of the rationality of individuals. Decision-contexts that arise in the strategic management of organisations could offer a rich, but so far under-utilised source of empirical anchoring points for the general theory of rationality, particularly with respect to competition & co-operation, identity, autonomy, and incremental action, as follows:

i) *Competition* Traditional game theory implicitly assumes *utility maximising* players, with consistent preferences for the formal game outcomes. Evidence of competitive and co-operative interactions between firms or organisations could now provide some empirical anchoring points for game-related theories, to complement the experimental gaming approach involving individuals as subjects (e.g., Plott, 1982; Colman, 1982). For example, empirical studies of competitive organisational interactions could potentially be used test hypotheses about *imperfectly*-rational agents, in general.

ii) *Autonomy & Identity* The *expressive* form of rationality (in **R**) involves experimentation with preferences and is therefore not capable of being reduced to *utility maximisation,* in which preferences are given and fixed. In the language of the following chapter, *expressive* rationality is not "*RUM* captured" (e.g. Hargreaves-Heap, 1989). This form prescribes (corporate) acts as simple expressions of (corporate) identity, or autonomous corporate values, rather than the maximisation of shareholder returns. For example, in the context of strategic business acquisitions, preservation of identity and autonomy of the various entities often assumes an over-riding importance, in the policy dialogue. In any environment of pervasive uncertainty, such strategies are indeed rational, but in a fundamentally different sense from means-ends plans (cf. Singer 1992).

Conclusion

The conceptual framework of "Strategy as Rationality" sees that developments in the general theory of rationality are, at the same time, contributing to a richer prescriptive theory of strategy, whilst much strategic management research has itself become directly relevant to the general theory of (individual or human) rationality. Empirical programs focusing on such issues as corporate competition and co-operation, organisational persistence, divisional autonomy and identity, are, at the same time, also tackling some of the more enduring problems of rationality.

Yet we are not finished. If strategy and rationality are indeed the same subject, both being concerned with quite general problems of action, decision and behaviour set in socio-economic contexts, then so too is ethics, morality and the broad discipline of moral philosophy. Accordingly, in the following chapter, the framework of strategy as rationality is extended to incorporate the moral dimension, thereby revealing strategic management and business ethics to be essentially the same subject. In more practical terms, there is now an imperative for the multiple types of strategic entity to contribute, together and directly, to the creation of desirable futures.

3. Strategy as morality

There is now a growing body of opinion, expressed most forcefully in the Business Ethics literature (e.g. Freeman, 1984; Goodpaster, 1988; Hosmer, 1991) that moral philosophy could inform strategic management in ways that complement or even supplant the contribution from Economics. Many corporate managers have expressed similar views. At a recent conference on the Ethics of Business in a Global Economy (in Columbus, Ohio, 1992) several quite famous CEO's were openly competing with each other...to express their social and environmental concerns. For example, Georges-Yves Kervern, of UAP, France, argued quite forcefully that a synthesis of corporate strategy with ethics is *Une therapeutic -la moins violente possible -des maladies de la societe."* Akio Morita, chairman of Sony similarly argued (on another occasion) that "Japanese corporations must start to think differently" not only increasing dividends but also "treating employees more humanely, whilst contributing more to the community and environmental protection".

In the USA, Ben & Jerry (icecream entrepreneurs) have repeatedly and publicly attributed their US$1bn p.a. turnover not to sophisticated competitive analysis, but to very high rates of new product introduction combined with egalitarian management policies of comparatively narrow salary differentials, luxury Creches, family leave and round-table decision-making. At the same time, private sector managers in many other countries are actively seeking ways of blending social justice with their quest for economic efficiency. One manager in New Zealand has hired new staff only from the long term unemployed, another public company has spent $50,000 on local public schools, in addition to paying tax. Finally, in the UK, the successful policies and practices of the Body

Shop, are not only well known, and respected, they are also widely copied. Most significantly, the "Body Shop" is said to be one of the most studied and discussed HBS cases ever.

If, as some believe, this sort of direct social action by corporate entities is a big mistake, because it reduces international competitiveness of business by adding to costs, then it is indeed a rather widespread abberation. Some economic and political theories would view this trend

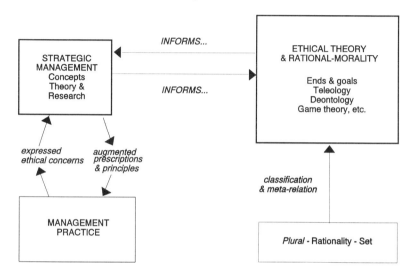

Figure 3.1 Strategy and ethics

as naive and mistaken, unless the socially oriented policies and practices really reflect nothing other than a public-relations or marketing *ploy* (e.g. Friedman, 1970). Others, however (e.g. Sen, 1977 & 1987, Goldman, 1980, Buchanan, 1985, Etzioni, 1988, Kuhn, 1992) have sought to justify such policies and missions indirectly, within a critical but rigorously argued *meta*-theory of conventional Economics. In this chapter, the Strategy-as-Rationality framework (chapter 2) is extended, in order to offer a justification of direct social and ethical engagement, beyond what is demanded by the market, but nonetheless within a prescriptive theory of strategic management (Figure 3.1 and 3.2).

To date, ethical concerns have not had much of a presence in the mainstream theory of strategic management. There are several possible explanations for this, as follows:

(i)   *"Strategy is about self-interest"*: To the extent that strategy is "how one goes about seeking personal gain" (Schendel, 1991) ethical-*egoism* constitutes the definitive moral foundation for strategy.   To the extent that moral philosophy then offers alternatives to egoism, or is critical of it, it becomes irrelevant.

(ii)   *"Strategy targets the powerful*: Strategy, as a discipline, targets the upper echelons (e.g. Hambrick & Mason, 1990) or those seeking power. In contrast, ethical concerns are sometimes seen as "an affliction of the weak" (e.g. Nietzche, 1886).

(iii)   *Strategy is practical*:   The discipline addresses the expressed concerns of practitioners, which are primarily commercial, legal and managerial; but not ethical.

(iv)   *Strategy is modern*:   Strategy addresses distinctively modern managerial problems; whereas moral philosophy is an ancient discipline.

All of these supposed justifications for an *a*-moral, or economically-rational conception of strategy have been cast into doubt by developments over the last couple of decades.   First, stakeholder, environmental and other social concerns have already entered many practical strategy frameworks (e.g. Andrews, 1980).   These concerns could reflect a significant extension of the "self-interest" component of strategy. Next, as described above and elsewhere (e.g. Moss-Kanter, 1991) many practicing C.E.O.s have expressed social, environmental and ethical concerns, in their words and actions.   Finally, the fact that moral philosophy is indeed an ancient discipline, does not mean that it should be forgotten.

Strategic goals and ethics

Many apparently ethical concerns, involving the well-being of other entities, are already firmly incorporated within the general theory of rationality. Indeed, the idea that the rationality of the individual has an important evaluative dimension, concerning an individual's choice of goals, or ends, was first mentioned in chapter 1. However, compared to the economically-oriented theories, moral philosophy and the other social sciences have paid much more attention to the precise nature and

31

optimal specification of goals (e.g. Etzioni, 1988, Rawls, 1972, Rescher 1993). It is no surprise, therefore, that the evaluative or moral dimension has not been forgotten in strategic management: it is already quite clearly and comprehensively mirrored in the mainstream theory. The correspondences concerning goals, or ends, are as follows:

1. **Rational-egoism ~ shareholder-value-creation.** Egoism involves satisfying one's own preferences (i.e. *utility maximisation*). If this is set in carefully specified market contexts, it formally yields Pareto-optimal outcomes. This result, in turn, is at the heart of the normative theory of shareholder value-creation. Assuming appropriate managerial reward and incentive structures are in place (e.g. stock options and other performance incentives) the concepts of egoism for individuals and value-creation for other strategic entities, such as firms and corporations, are very similar in terms of their origin, their behavioral implications and their ethical justification (e.g. Hosmer, 1991).

2. **Rational-sympathy ~ stakeholders-as-constraints.** Extended forms of ends-rationalities correspond with stakeholder approaches in strategic management. Both flow from the idea that it is rational (right, good) to have other goals in addition to self-interest, or shareholder value-creation, respectively. The "sympathy" form of extended individual rationality (Sen, 1977) corresponds precisely to Ansoff's (1965) stakeholders-as-constraints position. Both see that serving others interests is prudential and pragmatically necessary, en route to achieving egoist goals in the longer term.

3. **Rational commitment ~ not-for-profit.** In contrast, Sen's rational commitments by the individual involve counter-preferential choice, genuine utility loss, or altruism. This corresponds to the special ethos of a not-for-profit organisation. In these cases, there is an over-riding (but nevertheless rational) commitment to a non-financial cause (e.g., health provision, providing employment, aesthetics, etc).

These forms of ends-rationality are progressively increasing in sophistication. The next level of complexity moves beyond attempts to merely specify rational goals, towards an emphasis on the processes of goal formulation, as follows:

Table 3.1
Strategy and ethical concepts

STRATEGY CONCEPT	ETHICAL CONCEPT
OBJECTIVES, GOALS	*value, substantive, (Wertrationalitat)*
SHAREHOLDER-WEALTH with mgt.incentives	*self-interest egoism*
STAKEHOLDER APPROACH	*extended*
STAKEHOLDERS AS CONSTRAINTS	*sympathy, interdependent*
NOT-FOR PROFIT SERVICE ETHOS	*commitment, (altruism)*
VALUE-UNCERTAINTY in planning	*goal ambiguity in rational choice*
FORMULATING OBJECTIVES as process	*deliberative, reflective*
POLICY DIALOGUE as autonomous process, *Ringi*	*expressive concern for autonomy*
SOCIAL COST-BENEFIT-ANALYSIS	*utilitarianism*
FAIRNESS-GOALS, RIGHTS-POLICIES	*contractarianism*
STRATEGIC DUTY	*deontology*

4. **Deliberative rationality ~ formulating goals**. The Rawlsian notion of a rational individual deliberating on goals corresponds to the concept of a policy dialogue, or the political and organisational process of goal formulation under ambiguity (e.g. Quinn, 1977).

5. **Expressive rationality ~ continuous goal processes**. In the absence of a definitive goal, the search for individuals' goals is continuous and important, or rational, in its own right. It underpins a person's sense of autonomy (self management) which is of ultimate value, beyond what is normally considered as economic wealth. This applies to the expressively rational individual (Hargreaves-Heap, 1989) as it does to "rational" organisations.

6. **Systemic (posterior) rationality ~ emergent strategic vision**.
    Just as a rational person's goals emerge over time, as a function
    of historical experience and capabilities, so does the strategic
    vision of the firm. In contrast with calculated means-ends logic,
    posterior rationality (e.g., March, 1978) refers to the emergence
    of individual goals, over time, as a historical process. This form
    or rationality corresponds to the ways-means-ends recipe (or
    "logic") for competitive organisational strategy (Hayes, 1985).

7. **Ethical reasoning categories ~ strategic typology**. Finally,
    each of the major approaches to ethical reasoning lends itself
    directly to a distinctive corporate policy. Utilitarianism in ethics
    corresponds to the use of social cost-benefit analysis in strategic
    choice, whereby policies are enacted that are considered to
    provide the greatest good for the greatest number. This criterion
    has been used at times by many health enterprises required to
    operate "like businesses". Contractarian or Rawlsian strategies,
    on the other hand are ultimately driven by concerns of fairness
    and justice (Rawls, 1972, Freeman, 1984). Some organisations
    exist specifically to promote these ideals. Deontological or
    Kantian strategies recognise corporate duties, or simply doing
    what is right, even in situations where this runs counter to
    mainstream commercial considerations (Goodpaster, 1988, Singer
    and Van der Walt, 1987).

In sum, the language of goals in strategic management theory is simply
copied from an equivalent discourse on rational-morality, found within
the general theory of (individual) rationality. As with other elements and
relations within the rationality-set, this is surely no coincidence. Once
again, it is explained by the simple observation that the three subjects,
strategy, rationality and ethics are *all* grappling with quite universal
problems of action, decision and behaviour of strategic entities in their
social, economic and cultural contexts.

The extended framework

Although ethical theory tends to emphasise ends, or goals, whilst the
subject of rationality has focused more closely on best-means, the
distinction is rather opaque, given that means, ends and beliefs are
always inextricably intertwined. This is fully recognised within the

general theory of rationality and much of ethical theory. The multiple rationalities in the rationality-set **R** are intertwined with almost all of the major approaches to ethical reasoning, such as teleology, deontology and contractarianism. Furthermore developments in game-theory in the last couple of decades have reinforced these connections, by mapping out quite new pathways from the rationality of game players to their *de facto* morality.

Teleology and deontology

Teleological, or consequentialist ethics are closely associated with instrumental rationality, or choosing means to achieve known goals. These goals include the pursuit of self-interest (*egoism*) and the greatest good for the greatest number (*utilitarianism*). The rationality ~ ethics linkages in this case are quite transparent (e.g. Fumerton, 1990). Moreover, according to De George (1990, p 44) utilitarianism simply "describes what rational people do in making moral decisions".

It is also a description of what other strategic entities do, when they conduct a full socio-economic cost-benefit analysis, taking into account the interests of multiple stakeholders. Such utilitarian analysis could be conducted under the umbrella of policy guidelines (i.e. rule-utilitarianism) or else adopted to facilitate a specific, one-off decision (act-utilitarianism). In contrast, "a rationally operated company tries to maximise *its* good and minimise *its* bad." (De George, 1991) Thus, various forms of moral reasoning also describe the "rational" behaviour of various strategic entities. Just as we speak of corporate strategy, so we also have corporate-utilitarianism, or corporate-egoism, etc.

The role of rationality in an alternative, deontological ethics, is even more crucial. According to De George (1990, p66), the deontological tradition considers that "*being moral is the same as being rational*" and that "by analysing reason ...we find the key to morality". In this context "reason" and "rationality" are seen as incorporating conscious reflection and analysis. Moreover, such reflection leads inevitably to the categorical imperatives of the Kantian ethical tradition (i.e. the realisation that a moral agent should act according to universalizable principles). A similar concept of *intra*-personal "reflection" is also found in Rawls' concept of *deliberative* rationality which emphasises a form of distributive justice, or fairness in society.

Such deliberation and reflection within the minds of individuals corresponds directly to the processes of discussion and consensus found within other strategic entities, or collectivities (e.g. Boland et al. 1994).

35

Indeed, processes of consensus-seeking lie at the heart of emerging *post*-modernist conceptions of *contextual* rationality (e.g. Habermas, 1981), as well as in the ethical counterpart, the thesis of morals by agreement (Gautier, 1990). In sum, what is good for individuals, according to deontological traditions, is likewise good for all types of strategic entity.

Game theory

More recently, a variety of developments in game theory (*strategic belief* rationalities) have explained many aspects of apparently moral behaviour, using the language normally associated with forms of rationality. For example, the prisoner's dilemma game provides a clear and unambiguous rationale for obeying the Kantian categorical imperative, recasting this apparently "moral" principle as a form of rationality (e.g. Rapoport, 1991). Related work by Mackie (1978) offers rational game theoretic accounts of many principles of everyday, observed morality, such as returning favours. Also in this spirit, Axelrod (1984) used computers to explore the vast complexities of dynamic gaming, uncovering rational foundations for being nice and forgiving (typical moral language) as well as provocable and clear. In Axelrod's analysis, the game players themselves were disembodied, yet once again they have been repeatedly honoured elsewhere with a dual interpretation: as individuals (in Axelrod's own commentary) and as business firms, in the strategy literature (e.g. Nielsen, 1988; Singer, 1988).

Experimental gaming research, at the interface of Economics and Psychology has forged yet other pathways between rationality and moral reasoning. In these games, players' pay-offs depend on the beliefs of the other players (as distinct from their strategy). This has allowed the effects of guilt and gratitude to be introduced to the calculus of game-playing (e.g. Geanakoplos et al, 1989). In sum, as Williams (1985) has noted: "*It might turn out (that) we are committed to an ethical life...because we are rational agents.*" As new theoretical developments steadily unfold (e.g. McLennen, 1989) this remark becomes ever more salient. Moreover, it quite plainly applies with equal force to the "ethical life" of the rational corporation, or any strategic entity *A*. It is prompted, not by the definition of the agent, but by the many shared characteristics of rationality and morality.

The complete framework of Strategy as Morality may now be set out (Figure 3.2). First, in chapter two, the structured set **S** of strategic management concepts was placed in an isomorphic correspondence with the set **R** of *plural*-rationalities, implying a form of corporate-rational-agency. Next, the overall fabric of the *plural* rationalities is quite sufficient to wrap up much of practical morality and a very large part of a wider ethical theory. Together, these propositions lead to the conceptual framework of Strategy as Morality in which all strategic entities are re-cast as moral agents.

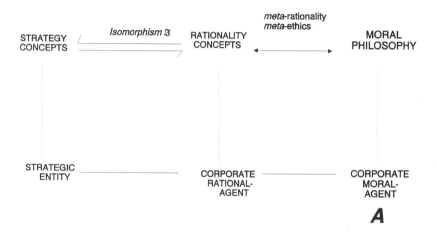

Figure 3.2 Strategy as morality

Like corporate rational agency (cf. Appendix 1) the idea of corporate or collective moral agency has also been repeatedly challenged. The tension between *pro-* and *anti*-moral-agency camps has at least equalled that between the opposing camps on rational-agency. The main arguments levelled against moral agency include: (i) the machine metaphor, (ii) descriptive ethics, and (iii) the diversionary argument. Like their counterparts in rationality, these independent challenges to corporate moral agency may also be seen as "roadblocks" in the path of inquiry, to be confronted accordingly (Appendix 2). This approach might be considered radical, maverick, or simply pragmatic: it undoubtedly opens the way to useful insights and usable methodologies. More importantly, it enables strategic management and business ethics to be seen and widely understood as not only related, but essentially the same subject!

Prescription in strategic management

The framework of Strategy-as-Moral-Philosophy propels the *plural* rationalities and ethics directly into a prescriptive theory of strategic management. First, within the new framework, strategy concepts may be evaluated with reference to various *meta*-rational and meta-ethical criteria, i.e. criteria for choosing rationalities and ethics. Next, the framework underpins a strategic decision-aid, SCIO. Finally, there are some broader and more general implications for strategic management practices.

Choosing rationalities and ethics

When managers use particular ways of thinking, concepts, techniques and models in formulating and implementing strategy, they are also, at the same time, making implicit choices between rational-moral principles. For example, a focus on such strategy concepts as stakeholders-as-constraints, continuous goal processes, etc., corresponds, within the framework, to an implicit choice of rationalities, (*sympathy, expressive*), in **R**. This raises a rather crucial question:

"Which rationalities and ethics should be used to prescribe strategy?"

In seeking an answer to the corresponding question about the rationalities of individuals, philosophers and social scientists have developed several *meta*-rational and *meta*-ethical criteria, for classifying and evaluating the *plural* rationalities $r \epsilon R$ (hence $s \epsilon S$) as follows:

(a) *AGGREGATE vs AGENT ORIENTATION*: Some rationalities have served as foundations of formal aggregate-level economic theories, associated with public-policy prescriptions (e.g. Thaler and Sheffrin, 1981, Russell and Thaler, 1985). These are the economic rationalities, $r \epsilon R^{EC}$. In contrast, some other $r \epsilon \overline{R}^{EC} \subset R$, e.g. *expressive, resolute, contextual*, are primarily oriented towards a localised decision-theory, more at the level of the individual (or corporate) agent. These forms emphasise some of

38

the more subtle dimensions of rationality, involving identity and co-ordination. These "agent-oriented" $r \in \overline{\mathbf{R}}^{EC}$ are, *prima facie*, at least as relevant to problems of strategy at the level of the firm, as the elements of the *economic*-rationality-set.

(b)   *RUM-CAPTURED vs ELUSIVE*:   Some of the $r \in \mathbf{R}$ may be "captured" by arguments that identify them, for at least some purposes, as special cases of *rational utility maximisation (RUM)*, or formal rank-ordering of preferences (e.g. Hirshleifer, 1976). Sen's *sympathy* or Etzioni's (1986) *interdependent* utility are partly captured within this net, as is *bounded* rationality, after allowing for the costs of information and computation. In terms of the present framework, *RUM* (not itself listed in Tables 2.1-2.6) is simply an umbrella-term, covering a subset $\mathbf{R}^{RUM} \subset \mathbf{R}$. The precise membership of this (fuzzy?) set is itself a matter to be settled through *meta*-rational argument. Other $r \in \mathbf{R}$ in contrast, are more "elusive". Examples include, *commitments, expressive, contextual* forms (Table 2). Within the present framework, the existence of these elusive forms implies that strategy should involve occasional (corporate) self-sacrifice; expression of (corporate) values; or the creation and maintenance of institutions and (corporate) traditions.

(c)   *TEMPORAL-ORIENTATION (Forward-looking vs. Backward -looking)*:   The forward-looking rationalities, $\mathbf{R}^{FOW} \subset \mathbf{R}$, are defined without reference to the past, whilst for $r \in \mathbf{R}^{BAK}$ there is at least some explicit historic reference. The set $\mathbf{R}^{BAK}$ includes: *posterior, adaptive, quasi, selected, resolute*, and *contextual* forms, amongst others. The partition $\mathbf{R} = \mathbf{R}^{BAK} \cup \mathbf{R}^{FOW}$ now underpins the broad strategy prescription of adapting to the past whilst, at the same time integrating with possible futures (Mintzberg, 1990; Ansoff, 1991; Kervern, 1990).

(d)   *META-ETHICAL SCOPE*   Several other *meta*-ethical criteria critically evaluate the scope of any given form of rationality, $r \in \mathbf{R}$, as follows:

Globally vs Locally Optimal (Mclennen, 1990).   A globally-optimising $r \in \mathbf{R}$ maximises total lifetime utility for the agent, after taking into account the impact of current decisions on the agent's future preferences, learning, habit-formation and co-ordination with others (*resolute* is global, narrow *egoism* is local).

Universalizable vs Exclusive (Kant, 1956). A universalizable r ϵ **R** is one that the agent prefers other agents to adopt (*Kantian* is universalizable, by definition, self-interest as *RUM* is not, in Prisoners' Dilemma Games).

Self-Supporting vs. Self-Defeating (Gautier, 1990). A self-supporting r ϵ **R** hypothetically chooses itself when used to select an r ϵ **R**, as in Figure 3.3. Whilst *Kantian* and *commitment* are self-supporting, in this sense, formal-*RUM* is self-defeating in the Prisoners' Dilemma.

Collectively, these and several other *meta*-criteria (perfect-imperfect; precision-of-definition, etc.) characterise the prescriptive gap that now separates the rationality assumptions of mainstream economic theory from several other normative principles of rationality and ethics. Put differently, whilst the axioms of *RUM* models in economics undoubtedly have a powerful normative appeal, so also do various *meta*-criteria that *RUM* fails. Now, with Strategy-as-Moral-Philosophy in place, these same *meta*-criteria could also be used to evaluate the corresponding strategy concepts, s ϵ **S**.

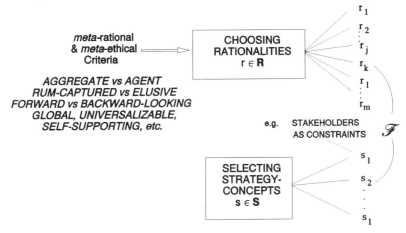

Figure 3.3 Meta-criteria for rationality and strategy concepts

For example, under the mapping $\Im$, defined in chapter two, the strategy concept of STAKEHOLDERS AS CONSTRAINTS, in **S**, corresponds to *rational sympathy* in **R**. As a form of rationality, the latter is: *Agent-oriented, RUM-captured* (utility could be maximised after allowing for the impact on others), also *forward-looking, local, non-universalizable*, and *self-defeating*. "STAKEHOLDERS AS CONSTRAINTS", in **S**, is thus characterised as a component of a general prescriptive theory of strategy, in exactly the same way. Put differently, it makes good sense to say that corporate strategy should be predicated on a view of stakeholders-as-constraints, but this sense of "should" is explicitly qualified by the *meta*-criteria.

The SCIO technique

In practical strategic thinking, these complexities and ambiguities surrounding the various *meta*-criteria, *meta*-relations and incomplete *meta*-rational arguments could be avoided, simply by appealing to all of the principles of *plural* rationality and ethics. To foster this sort of integrative multi-dimensional approach, a new strategic decision model or methodology is needed, which implicitly assumes all the plural rationalities. Finding such a "model" is simple: it is really nothing other than the Tables 2.1-2.6 (chapter 2) and Table 3.1, above. These tables may be used for developing a checklist, an *inquiry* procedure, SCIO, to structure a *plurally*-rational and hence also an ethical strategic decision process.

   "SCIO" stands for Specifying Canonical Issues and Options, with "canonical" simply meaning salient and comprehensive. (It also means "I know", in Latin, conveying the idea of strategic entities as knowledge and wisdom systems.) It is a structured inquiry methodology, similar in some ways to Cognitive Mapping (e.g. Rosenhead, 1989, Singer 1994d). However, it is more oriented towards available reasons, than shared beliefs. SCIO seeks to improve strategic analysis by directing attention to each distinctive dimension and form of rationality. In this way, factors such as histories and traditions, co-ordination with others, identities, rights and duties must all take their place in an expanded form of strategic thinking, alongside the more conventional economic and commercial considerations. Put differently, SCIO supports *strategic thinking without boundaries* (cf. Singer 1994b).

If answers to all the questions in Table 3.2 are pursued systematically, the resulting decision at least reflects an awareness of the fullest possible range of normatively relevant issues, at some procedural level within the strategic entity. With SCIO, the answers to the questions do not really matter! What does matter is the overall process of moving towards a

Table 3.2
SCIO: A systematic inquiry

1. Belief rationalities

1.1 *Belief:* Has *A* checked and verified all its relevant beliefs?

1.2 *Strategic:* Do *A*'s beliefs about future events allow for the reactions and interactions of other entities?

1.3 *Parametric:* Has *A* developed a myopic plan, assuming an unreactive environment?

1.4 *Extensive:* What are *A*'s expectations based upon historic and current data with extrapolation?

1.5 *Scientific, intensive:* What are *A*'s expectations or forecasts as determined by a formal model, or simulation, etc.?

1.6 *Perfect:*
   (i)   How complete or comprehensive is *A*'s knowledge?
   (ii)   How reliable are *A*'s predictions?

1.7 *Minimal:* Are *A*'s currently activated beliefs all mutually consistent?

2. Means Rationalities

2.1 *Instrumental:* Does *A* have a conventional means-ends plan, with an implementation program?

2.2 *Perfect, strong:* Has *A* calculated an optimal course of action?.

2.3 *Minimal (inference):* Has *A* actively searched for new inferences from the current beliefs?

2.4 *Intensive:* Has *A* developed and used a formal model-based strategy-selection system?

2.5 *Imperfect, procedural:* Has *A* developed decision-procedures and acceptability-criteria?

2.6 *Selective (2):* Is *A* achieving its current potential (e.g. with existing assets)?

2.7 *Bounded:* Has *A* explored ways of
   (i)   improving the allocation of attention,
   (ii)   reducing the costs of information search and processing?

2.8 *Quasi:* What would the majority of *A*'s decide if they were in this situation?

2.9   *Adaptive:* Does *A* carry out means-ends planning iteratively, continually learning and revising goals?

2.10   *Pre-commitment:* What action could *A* take now to prevent a possible and foreseeable change of goal or loss of commitment?

2.11   *Excess-of-Will:* Has *A* identified any subgoals whose direct pursuit could be counter-productive or impossible?

2.12   *Rational-postponement:* Has *A* reflected upon the value of waiting and of keeping options open?

3. Backward-looking (systemic) Rationalities

3.1   *Posterior:* What are *A*'s goals now? Should these be reformulated in the light of experience with past strategy.

3.2   *Resolute:* If current strategy fails to meet the updated criteria, was this situation foreseen in original evaluation of the strategy?

3.3   *Constrained:*
       (i)   Is completion of current project or strategy a long-standing unfulfilled mission of *A*? (ii) Is continuation of a current questionable strategy an opportunity for *A* to develop lasting habits (of task-completion) conferring future benefits?

3.4   *Ratchet:*
       (i)   What is the optimal timing and frequency of re-considerations?
       (ii)   Does a change of strategy now imply damage to *A*'s reputation, or violation of trust in *A*, or loss of *A*'s co-ordination with others?

3.5   *Retrospective:*
       (i)   If $\mathcal{P}+$ is changed, abandoned, will *A* be perceived (by *A* or others) as inconsistent? (ii) Can a justification of $\mathcal{P}-$ be communicated?
       (iii)   Have psychological biases (in forecasts for $\mathcal{P}+$) been allowed for?

3.6   *Open:*
       (i)   Have all mistakes in *A*'s past strategies been fully investigated and corrected?
       (ii)   Has *A* thoroughly reviewed its past behaviour and taken all corrective steps, revising procedures (and beliefs) appropriately?

3.7   *Natural:* Have *A*'s beliefs been revised appropriately to reflect *A*'s experiences?

3.8 *Selective (Systemic):*
    (i)   Will a habit and reputation of persistence (in similar situations) make *A* vulnerable to competitors with different strategies?

    (ii)   Is there a risk to *A* of a war-of-attrition (in the market for outputs of the current strategy?

3.8 *Deliberative:* Does current and future strategy utilise to the full *A*'s newly-learned capabilities (competencies, capacities) developed during past strategies?

3.9 *Contextual:* Is future strategy part of a mission that involves "the creation or maintenance of traditions and institutions that express *A*'s vision of the good life with others?"

4. Ends rationalities

4.1 *Ends, value-rationality:*
    (i)   What are *A*'s goals?
    (ii)   Why does *A* have these (stated) goals?
    (iii)   Are they the best goals?

4.2 *Egoism:* Is *A* pursuing its own interests?

4.3 *Extended ends-rationality:* Does *A* have goals other than self-interest?

4.4 *Sympathy:* Do *A*'s own "interests" include the interests of other entities *A*, *A*,...

4.5 *Rational-Commitments:* Is *A* making some altruistic choices in pursuit of others interests?

4.6 *Expressive:* Has *A* achieved a sense of autonomy by systemically re-evaluating its own goals?

4.7 *Deliberative:* Has *A* set up a procedure or policy dialogue for assessing its goals and reducing doubt about its goals?

5. Rational-Ethics

5.1 *Utilitarianism:* Is *A* seeking and producing the greatest good for the greatest number (of other entities)? Is *A* using a Social-Cost-Benefit approach?

5.2 *Contractarianism:* Does *A* have goals and policies involving fairness and protection of the rights of other entities (groups, individuals etc)?

5.3 *Deontology:* Does *A* fulfil all its duties and obligations?

6. Action & Expressive-rationality

6.1　*Action-rationality:* Is the strategy process in *A* conforming to the various principles of logical incrementalism (e.g. building awareness, overcoming opposition, partial solutions)?

6.2　*Expressive:* Is *A* taking actions that express its values and its own autonomous identity?

7. Other dimensions of rationality

7.1　*Interactive:* Does *A* look for possible rationales and patterns (over time) in its own and in other's decisions?

7.2　*Structural:* Has *A* determined the best structure of its own decision-making, with respect to:
　　(i)　　the involvement of subsystems
　　(ii)　identifying the issues
　　(iii)　distinguishing the phases?

broader wisdom and a balanced *Gestalt,* when determining the strategic direction. This is most appropriate, because the meta-rational arguments are not complete, so there is no analytic or calculable best solution to the optimal strategy problem. In contrast, conventional approaches to strategic option-evaluation are often quite naive in this respect. Managers and planners using conventional strategic and financial techniques are in effect choosing their own narrow or myopic form(s) of rationality, perhaps without ever realising it; that is, without realising that they are implicitly accepting some highly questionable *meta*-rational and *meta*-ethical arguments.

Further implications

In practice, the SCIO technique is but one of the potential spin-offs from strategy as morality. There are also implications for the design of management control systems and for the articulation of corporate missions. The decision making philosophy implicit in SCIO could quite readily be coupled to multi-criteria performance evaluation and incentive systems, rewarding behaviours such as learning from past mistakes (*open, systemic*), preparedness for a crisis (*minimising harm*), strong stakeholder relationships (*sympathy, commitments*), or the level of development of an identity (*expressive*), in addition to conventional *ex post* financial measures.

There are also much broader implications for the type of socially engaged business policies that were described earlier. To see this, it is helpful to draw a distinction between an old-game of strategy and a new-game. The "old game" was based squarely upon managerial-economics, with its implicit assumptions of rational *utility maximization*. It involved profit-maximising "firms", competing against each other, but subject to laws of a government of a nation state, or an empire.

However, in the new century (which began around 1975, according to Peter Drucker), with its transnational productive entities, industry networks, virtual-corporations, and stateless cyber-funds, the old game of strategy now seems unrealistic, or even dangerous. In the "new game", multiple types of strategic entity co-exist alongside governments and "economies" that do not even correspond to language-communities. If all these entities simply pursue their own interests, unrestrained by effective authority, we have something like the Hobbesian state of nature, but on a much more Global scale. Thus, the lives (of most of the entities themselves) inevitably become nasty, brutal and short, even as some others prosper greatly.

In the "new game" of strategy-as-morality, the basic rules are different from the old game. They may now be summarised as follows:

> *The things you should do as a strategic manager, acting on behalf of any of the types of strategic entity, are precisely the things you should do as an integrated and balanced person.*

For example all strategic entities will have to learn, develop capabilities and consider how their actions might evoke a response from others. In addition they will also have significant ambition or "strategic intent" and take into account the interests of all other entities, including those entities that do not have control of the new-game info-wealth. This means that all strategic entities must engage in some pragmatic service to other entities, at least partly in accordance with their needs, but independently of their ability to pay.

This is exactly what many enlightened businesses have been doing, for some time. In the new game, which many around the World are now learning to play, or at least think about, the retreating Welfare States of the old game must become joined and buttressed by multiple *welfare-entities*. Even "private" companies will learn to play the new game, as they develop to the level of strategy-as-morality. The necessary transition from the old game to the new game will involve not only changes in rationalities and changes in language, it will also incorporate necessary changes in the nature and type of formal models used to support strategic decisions. The latter is the main focus of the next few chapters.

4. Reconciliations

The SCIO technique (Chapter 3) is a distinctive approach to supporting or aiding strategic decisions, rooted in *plural* rationality. It contrasts greatly with traditional model-based forms of strategic and financial analysis. Financial analysis often involves the use of cashflow forecasts and probabilities, combined within a formal model, like net present value (NPV) amd its variants (ENPV, CAPM, Option-Valuation, etc.). Strategic analysis, on the other hand, often involves simple graphical models, matrices, or heuristic decision aids. Thus, there is a rather crucial questions about models, arising in conjunction with the earlier question about choice of rationalities. In short, one must ask: *Which models are correct?*

In this chapter, the framework of "Strategy as Rationality" is extended to an analysis conflicting model-based appraisals of strategic options. Put differently, it becomes a framework for *meta-modelling*. With the adapted framework, model-based prescriptions are analysed at three levels: at the first level are the decision-models and techniques themselves, together with the questions that frequently arise in theory and practice about their inter-relationships. At the second level are the forms of rationality implicit in the models and their use. At the third level are the various *meta*-rational criteria and arguments.

More specifically, the framework combines the concepts of *plural*-rationality and meta-rational arguments with the concept of the *decision-function-rationalities* of models (originally due to Morecroft, 1983). It is then operationalised as a set of diagnostics, like SCIO, that evoke the deeper philosophical roots of conflicting model-based strategy prescriptions. Furthermore, by identifying the incomplete or more problematic metarational arguments, it then becomes possible to identify situations where additional model-based analysis is unlikely to be worthwhile.

An extended framework

The concept of conflicting model-based prescriptions for strategic decisions is illustrated in Figure 4.1. In the context of special investment opportunities, or a routine strategic review, various alternative strategies or investment projects $\mathcal{P}_1$, $\mathcal{P}^{ALT1}$,...., $\mathcal{P}^{ALT\ N}$ might be considered (e.g., *status-quo*, capacity expansion, foreign acquisition, divestment, a major R&D effort, increased marketing expenditure, etc.). Taken together, the projects or options comprise a set:

$$\{\mathcal{P}_1, \mathcal{P}^{ALT1},...., \mathcal{P}^{ALT\ N}\}$$

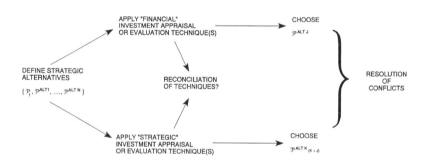

Figure 4.1. Conflicting prescriptions for strategic investments

To faciliate appraisals, planners could use various financial analysis models, from a set of models $\{m_1,.....,m_L\}$, such as the CAPM with probabilistic multi-period returns-forecasts, options-valuation models, or other quantitative techniques. They might also employ strategic (qualitative or heuristic) models, from another set $\{m_1',.....,m_n'\}$, such as the Boston Consulting Group (BCG) portfolio matrices, or "PIMS" principles, or, simply refer to broad policy guidelines, expressed in

49

natural (i.e. non-mathematical) language, such as "internal development, not acquisitions".

When more than one of these models, techniques, guidelines and principles are used to analyse the same investment proposal, conflicting prescriptions can easily result. Accordingly, questions have often been asked about whether such conflicts can ultimately be resolved, or how the model-based techniques and other principles might ultimately be reconciled (e.g. Myers, 1984, Pinches, 1982, in finance, Bettis, 1983, Bowman, 1980, Cooke, 1985 and Wensley, 1981, in strategy). The framework of strategy as rationality, extended to embrace the concept of decision-function-rationality, now provides an answer.

Decision-function-rationality

The concept of the decision-function-rationality (DFR) of a formal model is originally due to Morecroft (1983). The DFR of any given decision-model is the particular form of rationality implicit in the model or dislayed by the model user. More formally, the decision-function -rationality, ∂ (m), of any model m ϵ **M** (the set of models), is a mapping that associates any given model m with its underlying form(s) of rationality, $r_1^m \epsilon$ **R**. Thus, for any given model, m ϵ **M**, we have

$$\partial (m) = \{ r_1^m, r_2^m, , r_k^m \} \subset \mathbf{R}$$

For example, strategy models such as the BCG growth-share-matrix (e.g. Day, 1986), the Capital Asset Pricing Model (e.g. Naylor and Tapon, 1982), Social Cost-Benefit Analysis (e.g. Prest et al, 1965) are each mapped as follows:

$$\partial \text{ (BCG)} = \{ \text{strategic-beliefs, imperfect} \}$$
$$\partial \text{ (CAPM)} = \{ \text{RUM} \}$$
$$\partial \text{ (CBA)} = \{ \text{Act-utilitarianism} \} \text{ etc.}$$

In chapter three, various *meta*-rational or *meta*-ethical criteria, such as *aggregate-agent, rum-captured, temporal-orientation,* etc. were mentioned in connection with the problem of "choosing rationalities". Now it may be seen that a rather similar approach also applies to evaluating and choosing amongst formal strategy models (Figure 4.2).

Specifically, in the framework of Figure 4.2, the prescriptive status of any given formal model is equated with the status of its decision-

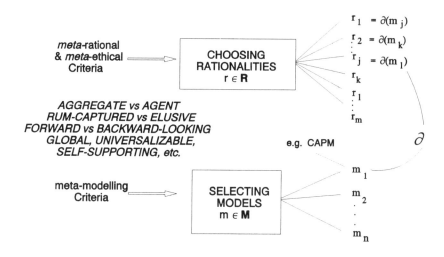

Figure 4.2. Choosing models and rationalities

function-rationality, $r \in \mathbf{R}$, relative to the meta-criteria (Figure 4.2). Thus, for example, the CAPM identifies investments that should be made, but only within a sense of "should" that is qualified by the *meta*-criteria as they apply to *RUM*. Some rather similar rational-ethical approaches to model evaluation (*meta*-modelling) have been proposed before, by Morecroft (1983), Myers (1984), Eilon, (1985), Van Gigch (1990) and Singer (1991).

Meta-rationality and models

Once the DFRs of conflicting models and principles are identified, the relationship between any given models or techniques may be partly characterised in terms of the philosophical arguments, mathematical results and empirical findings that place the corresponding forms of rationality relative to one another These include the criteria introduced in chapter 3, of *aggregate-vs. agent orientation, RUM-capture, temporal orientation, precision of definition and meta-ethical scope.*

For present purposes, it is not necessary to explore any of these meta-rational arguments or criteria in much depth. (This is done in the various source references throughout the book). It is simply sufficient to note that, finding or constructing a metarational argument may be

51

relatively easy in some cases, as with *bounded* versus *perfect* forms, or relatively difficult, as in the case of placing *strategic* beliefs within *substantive* rationality (game theory). Other relatively "easy" metarational arguments involve *sympathy* and *egoism, precommitment* and *perfect* forms, and to some extent *beliefs* about controllability and causality. Harder cases include some further aspects of beliefs about causality and strategic interdependence, rational *commitments, systemic* versus calculated forms, *expressive* rationality and *non-consequentialist* moral principles versus *utility maximisation* (i.e. meta-ethics).

The "difficulty" of a metarational argument need not be precisely defined for present purposes, but is generally determined by the existence of paradoxes, infinite regresses, disputed definitions, context effects, learning, or other partly unresolved philosophical arguments and ambiguous experimental findings within the general theory of rationality. This distinction between the "easier" versus "harder" (or relatively complete versus incomplete) metarational arguments is the final component of the extended framework (Figure 4.3). This distinction corresponds, via the DFR mapping, to having relatively favourable versus unfavourable prospects for reconciling prescriptions through further model-based analysis.

In cases where "easier" arguments apply to the relevant DFRs, further analysis, information search, or the refinement of heuristics is prescribed by the framework. However, where conflicts correspond via DFR to the harder metarational arguments, there are some more fundamental issues involved. Therefore, for these cases, further analysis in practice is unlikely to resolve the conflict, nor reconcile the models.

Diagnostics

The abstract represention of conflicting strategy prescriptions yields a practical methodology, involving a set of diagnostic questions. Table 4.1 sets out a variant of SCIO (chapter 3) that emerges naturally from the framework in Figure 4.3.

These diagnostic questions indicate directions for reconciling conflicting model-based prescriptions. The same diagnostics could also be used simply to systematically qualify any particular model-based financial or strategic analysis (e.g. Singer, 1986).

Decision support systems

The issue of alternative and conflicting model-based forms of analysis

52

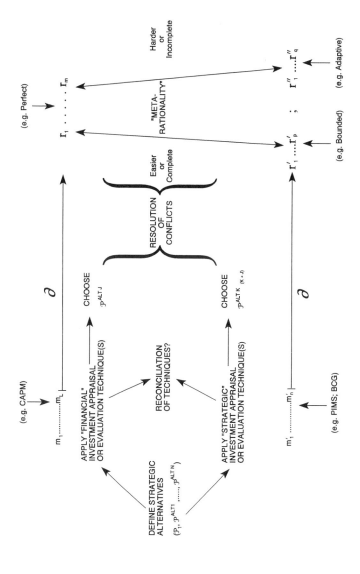

Figure 4.3. A conceptual framework for resolving conflicting model-based prescriptions

has also frequently surfaced in the specialised decision-support-system (DSS) literature. For example, spreadsheets linked to NPV criteria have been contrasted with intelligent management systems (e.g. Finlay, 1989) involving scenario generation and techniques for structuring and organising information, much of which cannot easily be incorporated into a spreadsheet financial analysis of a strategic option. Accordingly, designers of "intelligent" systems have sought to support the modes of thought with which users feel comfortable, rather than force a particular form of rationality upon the user. The framework of *plural* rationality and incomplete meta-rational arguments provides a theoretical justification for such a design philosophy. In addition, it also points to some specific loci for system-user's judgements and intuitions, or "right-mindedness" (e.g. Singer, 1981) as follows:

(i)   *Strategic Goals*: Meta-rational arguments involving goals (chapter 3) suggest that goals of a strategic entity cannot be ranked with reference to any definitive ideal. Accordingly, a DSS should not seek to impose a particular goal on users, but could instead help user(s) to consider or reconsider their own goals more carefully. Reports on actual experiences to date with implementing strategic-level DSS fit well with this particular prescription.

Table 4.1
Diagnostics evoking meta-rational arguments

To resolve conflicting prescriptions or qualify financial appraisals, consider:	Diagnostic evokes a Metarational Argument Concerning:
Q1. Are (various factors) incorporated into forecasts of key-performance-parameters (ROI, NPV etc.)?	
Q2. Are (various factors) considered before or after the strategic decision?	*Bounded rationality*
Q3. Are the (heuristic) rules appropriate in this context?	
Q4. Which causal or statistical relationships have been employed?	

Q5.	Are stakeholder's interests and reactions considered?	*Extended rationality (sympathy)*
Q6.	Is the investment construed and evaluated as a precommitment?	*Weakness of will and precommitment*
Q7.	Have any important factors been overlooked	*Minimal rationality*
Q8.	Which factors have been construed as controllable, or capable of being influenced?	*Belief rationalities*
Q9.	Are <u>conditional</u> forecasts used?	
Q10.	Have multilateral (game theoretic) situations been identified?	*Strategic beliefs (multilaterality)*
Q11.	Is the strategic analysis based on managerial self-interest (vs. a genuine commitment to "shareholder value")	*Extended rationality (commitment)*
Q12.	Is the strategic analysis based on some (other) commitment?	
Q13.	Is (corporate) tradition or culture a factor?	*Systemic forms*
Q14.	Are non-consequentialist ethical principles involved?	*Moral principles deontology)*
Q15.	Are subjective probabilities appropriate for this problem?	*Probabilistic beliefs*
Q16.	Do subjective probabilities (if used) reflect sufficient knowledge?	
Q17.	Have appropriate techniques been used to assess the reliability of information?	*Truth-values*

(ii) *Strategic Means*: Arguments involving means-rationalities suggest that a primary role of strategic-level DSS should be to overcome cognitive limitations of the user, rather than optimisation of outcomes based upon conditional forecasts. Put differently, the role of the DSS should be to sharpen-up the users' mental models. More specifically, DSS should (i) facilitate a re-examination of the causal and statistical relationships understood by the user, (ii) detect and eliminate inconsistent beliefs (iii) facilite appropriate inferences and (iv) locate and activate relevant knowledge. This prescription, of course, also fits very well with what has been learnt to date from actual experiences with DSS. It is further explored in the following chapter.

(iii)   *Other intuitive tasks*: Incomplete metarational arguments are also at the heart of conflicts involving (i) predictions of the strategic moves of other entities (ii) the impact of organisational traditions and cultures (iii) duties and obligations (iv) the valuation of options like creating a strategic window (v) assessing the reliability or truth value of items of intelligence information.

Conclusion

Previous treatments of the issue of conflicting model-based prescriptions have been quite varied. Such conflicts have been considered paradoxical (e.g. Bowman, 1980, Wensley, 1981) and as a technical challenge (e.g. Myers, 1988, Pinches, 1982). However, where conflicts occur in practice, they can also be seen as an opportunity for improving decision procedures, since they draw attention to the fallibility of any particular technique, model, theory or world-view (*Weltanschauung*). Such conflicts can provide the psychological motivation as well as the political justification for digging more deeply into a strategic problem. Yet, the further one digs, the more is becomes apparent that alternative methodologies, like SCIO, are needed to support strategic decision making, within a "new game" of strategy. New methodologies bring new rationalities and expanded ideologies, thus redirecting strategic thought and action. The following chapter continues an exploration of this theme.

5. Adaptations and transitions

The problem of conflict between strategic and financial analysis, considered in chapter 4 as a manifestation of meta-rational arguments, can also be viewed in terms of processes of adaptation and transition. That is, adaptation of the models themselves, with accompanying transitions to alternative problem-structuring methodologies. Rather than argue for outright abandonment of forecast-based DCF models, the present chapter therefore sets out some ways of adapting them, in order to facilitate a transition to the *plural* rationality of the strategic entity.

For more than a decade, the conventional application of DCF models to strategic investment decisions has been extensively criticised (e.g. Derkenderen & Crum, 1979, Hayes, 1985, Marsh et al, 1988, Rosenhead, 1989). Most of the critiques have centred upon the impossibility of producing the reliable forecasts needed for any conventional DCF analysis. However, in defiance of the critique, there has actually been a steady increase in the reported use of DCF in corporations (e.g. Klammer, 1984, Singer, 1985, Pike, 1988 *et seq,* Patterson, 1989). For example, a forestry division of one large diversified corporation, still, in 1994, values its plantings by extrapolating historical price trends forward 20 years, then calculating NPVs, despite the fact that such forecasts are "bound to be wrong" (e.g. Rosenhead, 1989).

This situation could be quite readily explained with reference to the many unorthodox uses of formal models in organisations, that have been observed by behavioral researchers (Table 5.1). Such models are sometimes used as rituals, akin to magical rites, sometimes as status-symbols, or else as pliers, used to extract confessions about subordinates' assumptions. In addition, Mintzberg (1993) has drawn attention to yet another important role that formal models or plans play: persuading influential outsiders, particularly the suppliers of finance.

In the adaptations of DCF described in this chapter (cf. Singer 1994) formal DCF models, with the associated financial-economic theory, are seen in the new way recommended in several recent OR-MS articles: simply as platforms for organised discussion, round tables, devices for evoking knowledge from memory, or catalysts for interdisciplinary bconversations (e.g. Bennett et al, 1982, Smith, 1993, Roy, 1993, Mahoney, 1993).

Table 5.1
Unorthodox roles of formal models in the strategy process

Formal models act as...

RITUALS ... reinforcing a culture of (strong instrumental) rationality, or sustaining and orientation towards a goal of value creation (Gimpl & Dakin, 1984).

GLUE ... binding or uniting managers behind a common set of concepts, practices, goals or strategies (Langley, 1991).

BATTERIES ... a source of motivation. Analysis per se acts psychologically to increase involvement and commitment and to reduce perceived risk (Langer, 1975).

STATUS-SYMBOLS ... access to the calculations displays status in the organization. This has also been observed with economic forecasts "used" in strategic analysis (Eerola, 1989).

PLIERS ... they are used to extract confessions from subordinates concerning their assumptions about strategy, or to squeeze subordinates into line when they oppose the strategy of the dominant coalition (Marsh et al, 1988).

The main criticism of traditional DCF use concerns the difficulty or even the impossibility of forecasting the cashflows that are conditional upon a project or proposal $\mathcal{P}$ and its alternatives $\mathcal{P}^{ALT1}$, $\mathcal{P}^{ALT2}$, ..., $\mathcal{P}^{ALTN}$. This problem of forecasting over a typical 3+ year planning horizon shows no signs at all of being solved. On the contrary, the continuing search for more reliable forecasting techniques has so far been conspicuously unsuccessful. At the same time, several independent research streams have now converged towards the same basically negative conclusion about the prospects for producing the kind of reliable cashflow forecasts needed as inputs for meaningful DCF calculations. They include:

(i)   Direct evidence and experience (e.g. Ang et al, 1979, Pinches, 1982, Crum et al, 1986, Patterson, 1989),

(ii)   *Meta*-forecasting research, (Makridakis, 1988),

(iii)   *Meta*-modelling theory, (e.g. De Geus, 1992, Van Gigch, 1991, Mehrez et al, 1989),

(iv)   Paradoxes of rationality, (e.g. Michael, 1989, Doktor et al, 1988, Singer, 1984, 1990, 1993) and

(v)   Chaos theory (e.g. Gleick, 1987, Feichtinger et al, 1993, Baumol, 1987 & 1989, Brock, 1993).

All of these areas of research have converged upon one main point, perhaps expressed most succinctly by Rosenhead (1989), that forecasts of the type needed for DCF analysis are "bound to be wrong". Thus, the experienced "difficulty" of incorporating strategic issues into cashflow forecasts may now itself be explained, and even predicted scientifically. Accordingly, as the phenomenon of un-forecastability has become more widely understood and appreciated, planners and strategy researchers have begun to shift their focus away from concepts of prediction and probability, towards alternative forecast -free forms of strategic analysis (e.g. Robinson, 1988).

Forecast-free methodologies

There are several methodologies of strategic analysis that do not require forecasts as inputs. These "forecast-free" methodologies include the content-oriented strategy techniques, such as BCG matrices, PIMS relationships, Industry-Attractiveness-Model, and others summarised in Prescott & Grant (1988) as well as the various process-oriented methodologies summarised in Rosenhead (1989). It is generally understood that these must all be used with care, as one might use ordinary mnemonics, rather than treating them as proven facts or algorithms. Some of these methodologies, like the SCIO technique (chapter 3) are purely qualitative (Table 5.2), involving no formal mathematical model at all, whilst others involve formal models, but not forecasts (Table 5.3).

Table 5.2
Qualitative forecast-free methodologies

DA-SAST is based upon the idea of stimulating access to stored knowledge, by juxtaposing conflicting perspectives. Evoked ideas are tested for consistency and relevance to the strategic problem. (Mason & Mitroff, 1981).

STRATEGIC CHOICE concerns the structuring of inter-related decision-problems, particularly in public-sector contexts. The environment, values, and the inter-relatedness of decisions are each regarded as areas of gross uncertainty. An incremental approach is advocated that involves switching between content-oriented and process-oriented modes of management. (Friend & Hickling, 1987).

SODA emphasises the achievement of consensus and commitment towards a course of action. The related technique of cognitive mapping involves making explicit a network of connected ideas. Elicited meanings are clarified by identifying a contrasting idea and are recorded in a way that orients them towards managerial actions (Eden, 1989).

Table 5.3
Quantitative forecast-free methodologies

PARE sets out a way of estimating a firm's unrealised potential and its ability to cope with adversity. These measures are regarded as determinants of fundamental economic value. The value of a strategic investment may then be assessed indirectly in terms of its impact on the firm's potential and resilience (Derkenderen & Crum, 1979).

ICM sets out a way of measuring the level of competitiveness of a firm. The methodology yields model-based prescriptions for broad classes of strategic investments, such as cost-reduction versus asset-renewal. With the ICM methodology, estimates of actual and potential performance of the firm and its competitor(s) are used as inputs, in place of forecasts (Oral, 1987).

ROBUSTNESS Analysis is a method for measuring the relative flexibility of strategic options, whilst at the same time recognising that such flexibility is itself but one of several criteria (Rosenhead, 1989).

In applications, particular strategy mnemonics and structuring methods are normally chosen by analysts or managers, for application to a given strategic problem, or set of problems. Thus, concealed within the strategic analysis there is a quite explicit meta-modelling decision, or choice of methodology. With DCF use, however, the situation is quite different. In most cases the DCF methodology is already firmly in place, embedded within the managerial minds and in the routines of the strategic entity *A*. Given this embeddedness of the DCF model, any proposal to totally abandon it, in favour of forecast-free alternatives (a meta-modelling decision) is itself bound to encounter resistance, or status quo bias (see chapter 6).

Adaptations

One practical way forward is to retain the DCF model but to adapt it. More specifically, *one could continue to attempt to prepare the needed cashflow forecasts, as if they were reliable and credible, but without actually believing them.* Such fake-forecasting, or *FAKE-CASTING*, then becomes nothing more than a procedure for evoking relevant contextual knowledge (Figure 5.1) and relevant theoretical knowledge (Figure 5.2) from memory, thereby improving the conceptual model of the strategic problem. With this "round table" perspective on the use of DCF, the formal models do not generate prescriptions. They do not tell you which projects are, in traditional language, "worthwhile"; rather, their primary purpose is to enable the strategic entity *A* to learn (Rosenhead, 1989, Morecroft, 1992, De Geus, 1992) or to improve shared understanding of the strategic situation (Oral et al, 1993).

In any particular case, the knowledge evoked by the "fake-casting" approach to estimating relevant cashflows, ostensibly for a DCF analysis, could involve either (a) the contextual details of the specific project and its environment (Figure 5.1), or else (b) technical theoretical knowledge, the generic issues (e.g. reputation, motivation, synergies, etc.) that have already been identified, within the underlying refined financial economic theory (Figure 5.2).

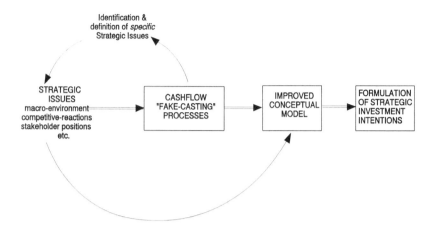

Figure 5.1   Fake-casting and context-specific issues

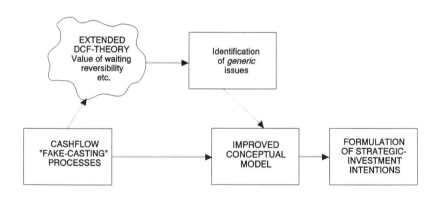

Figure 5.2   Fake-casting and generic issues

With context-specific fakecasting, the faked attempt to forecast cashflows over a typical 3+ year horizon simply serves to direct attention to a whole host of specific strategic issues. These, in turn, combine with independently identified macro-environmental and competitive issues, to enrich and improve the conceptual model. Investment intentions could then emerge from a generalised process of conflict management within *A*, the entity (as discussed further in chapter 8). With the latter "generic" approach to fake-casting (Figure 5.2) the DCF model with its underlying theory simply becomes evocative of pre-packaged theoretical understandings and conceptual categories. The following chapter (chapter 6) illustrates "generic" fakecasting, with reference to theories of investment with sunk costs.

Sub-optimising

There is another, quite different approach to adapting DCF methodology. This involves confinement of the model to particular types of decision, but also using it in conjunction with other criteria. In this case, it is necessary to refer to a basic distinction between two types of decision by any strategic entity *A*, "strategic *versus* other" decisions. This distinction has been identified many times in the meta-theories of forecasting, modelling, rationality and strategy, as follows:

STRATEGIC DECISIONS *are… "ill-defined, ill-structured, unstructured, unprogrammed, wicked, ambiguous, unclear, systemic, intuitive, incremental, inductive, human, practical, real-life,* PRIMARY MESSES *or* CONUNDRUMS*",*

whereas…

OTHER DECISIONS *are… "well-defined, well-structured, structured, programmed, tame, unambiguous, clear, mechanical, analytic, formal, deductive, mechanistic, technical, formal,* SECONDARY PROBLEMS *or* PUZZLES.

The "primary *versus* secondary" designation (Langley, 1991) in particular, has direct implications for the use of DCF. Whilst "strategic" decisions can be supported with the forecast-free methodologies, including fakecasting, DCF could still be applied in the more traditional way, to some "other" types of decision (Figure 5.3). However, in these secondary decision contexts, some changes to the criterion for investment (NPV >0) are now needed. To see this, it is first helpful to more fully characterise two types of investment decision, *TYPE 1* and *TYPE 2*, as follows:

TYPE 1 is a strategic decision to invest in some broad class of assets (it is helpful to think of a *set*, **A**) like new plant technology, as opposed to some non-investment strategy like a cost-reduction program.

TYPE 2 is a selection of a particular asset a_1 from a set **A** of technologically similar assets having known performance parameters.

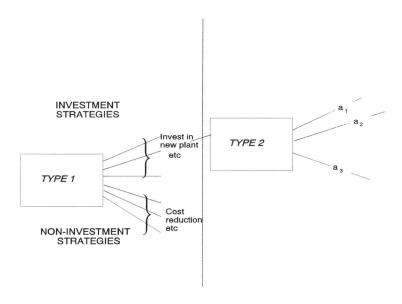

Figure 5.3 Two types of investment decision

In *TYPE 1* investment decisions, forecast-free problem structuring methodologies are needed. In *TYPE 2* "investment decisions", however, one is simply confronted with a variant of the classical capital budgeting problem for mutually-exclusive assets $a_1, a_2, \ldots, a_n$. Some adaptation of the traditional DCF decision-rules is then necessary, because the decision to invest in at least one asset a ϵ **A** has already been taken. In addition, there will always be other, non-financial criteria also applicable to the secondary asset-selection decision.

To illustrate, consider the case of an automotive manufacturing company whose fashionable product is quite deliberately priced too low, so that there is a long waiting list. Following a primary investment decision to expand capacity, managers are then faced with a selection from various available plant extensions. Each type of new plant has known technological parameters, known operating costs, and financing packages. A *sub*-optimizing DCF calculation simply combines these known operating and financing data, for each alternative, into a single basis for ranking...other things being equal. Then, following this exercise, other criteria, such as the preferences of the company's engineers, alternative uses of the different types of plant, quality of service support, etc. could also be brought into the analysis, perhaps within a formal multi-criteria (MCDM) framework. It has long been appreciated that it is simply impossible to subsume such factors as "quality" into reliable cashflow forecasts (e.g. Derkenderen & Crum, 1979, Singer 1986).

Transitions

The adaptations of DCF set out in the previous section, fake-casting and sub-optimisation, indicate just two possible approaches to facilitating transitions between old and new methodologies, with their associated ideologies. To date, such methodological and ideological transitions *per se* have received little attention in the social, managerial and policy sciences (e.g. Zeleny, 1990). Thus, these two adaptations of DCF could themselves now act as a "platform", or a "catalyst" for further productive *meta*-theorizing about the processes of ideological transition. The general relationship between adapted methodologies and ideological transitions can itself be made more explicit, again by using the concept of decision-function rationality, defined earlier (chapter 4) as a mapping from the set of formal models to the set of their underlying rationalities,

$$\partial : \mathbf{M} \Rightarrow \mathbf{R}.$$

In the case of the traditional DCF, the *rational utility maximisation (RUM)* of neoclassical economics is the implicit form. In contrast, the adaptations of DCF and the other forecast-free methodologies in Tables 5.2 & 5.3 correspond, *via* the mapping ∂, to other form(s) of rationality, or to a *plural* rationality. The transition from conventional DCF methodology towards the alternatives may therefore be characterised, at least partially, as a transition from a narrow economic rationality to *plural* rationality.

Within the framework of "strategy as rationality", this becomes characterised as a transition from a narrow strategy of shareholder value-creation, towards a much more pluralistic strategic management ideology. In the latter, considerations of co-ordination, persistence, potential, autonomy and identity, reputation, multiple-values and ethics,

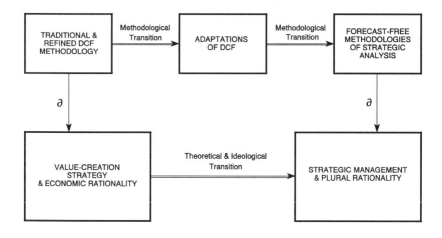

Figure 5.4 Methodological and ideological transitions

many of which resist *RUM-capture* (chapter 3) all become an integral part of the conceptual models within the strategic entity *A*. In the following chapter, this type of pluralistic strategic wisdom is applied to the problem of investment decisions involving sunk costs. In these vexed situations, strategic entities must simply balance the forward-looking forms of rationality against the backward-looking forms.

6. Reconsiderations

There is an abundance of compelling evidence that all types of strategic entity (e.g. individuals, firms, nations, etc.) often act, intend to act, or desire to act in ways that depend upon their own past actions, intentions, plans or strategies. Examples of this dependence have been identified and analysed, across the entire spectrum of the social, economic, cognitive and biological sciences, as well as in philosophical inquiries (e.g. Staw, 1976, Kahneman & Tversky, 1981, Thaler, 1985, Dawkins 1980, Kavka, 1983).

Although the special problems posed for corporate managers in situations involving large sunk costs have also been explored before (e.g. White, 1986, Bowen, 1987, Schwenk et al 1989, Bateman, 1989, and others), they have never been satisfactorily resolved. The conceptual framework of Strategy-as-Rationality now enables some significant progress in the analysis of this problem. First, it is necessary to state, in simple but formal terms, a generic sunk-cost problem as follows (refer Figure 6.1).

(i)   The strategic entity A is a plurally-rational agent.

(ii) $\mathcal{P}$ is a project, plan, program, or strategy that is being re-considered by A, at some time, t_n.   Part of $\mathcal{P}$ (i.e. $\mathcal{P}-$) has already been implemented.   Continuation with the next part of $\mathcal{P}$ (i.e. $\mathcal{P}+$) is re-considered.   Thus, A will either continue with $\mathcal{P}$ (i.e. choose $\mathcal{P}+$) or else abandon $\mathcal{P}$ thereby choosing an alternative, [not $\mathcal{P}+$] with $\mathcal{P}^{ALT}$

Thus, for example, in the case of A as a nation or group of nations, "$\mathcal{P}$" could be a power-generation scheme (Singer 1993). In the case of A as a corporation, P could be the construction of a large manufacturing plant with specified technology. With *A* interpreted as an individual, P could be a simple plan to go to a basketball match (e.g. Thaler, 1985); or with *A* as a humble digger - wasp (Dawkins, 1980) P could simply be a strategy of fighting challengers in the population of wasps until they surrender, in order to acquire a well-provisioned nest. So far as the understanding of sunk costs is concerned, "Strategy as Rationality" sees these as *isomorphic* problems, sharing many salient characteristics.

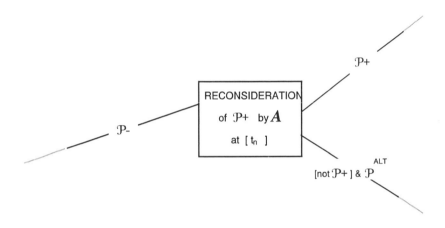

Figure 6.1   The generic sunk cost problem

Theory-types

There are already at least three types of theory that could be applied to the generic sunk cost problem: normative, descriptive and hybrid. *Normative* theory, is a family of models $\mathbf{M}^{\text{NORM}}$ built around assumptions of *utility-maximising*. The models in this type of theory are mostly *content*-oriented, working through the "normative" implications of factors like reputation, competition, risk and reversibility, etc. Financial Economic models are in this class, along with the variants of the subjective-expected-utility (SEU) model in decision-theory. The prescriptions derived from $\mathbf{M}^{\text{NORM}}$ comprise another set, $\mathbf{P}^{\text{NORM}}$ (Figure 6.2).

Descriptive theory is a family of models $\mathbf{M}^{\text{DESC}}$ built around empirical data. These are process-oriented, concerned with *what A* decides and *how* it decides, e.g. what heuristics are used and what is attended to. Social Psychological and Cognitive Psychological models are all in this class. *Hybrid* theories then combine elements of normative with descriptive theory. For example, empirical, data-driven variants of the SEU model, like Prospect Theory (Kahneman & Tverky, 1979) and Transaction Utility Theory (Thaler, 1985) are "hybrids". They include an analysis of sunk costs and they have been used as foundations for developing prescriptions at the aggregate economic or public-policy level (Russell et al, 1989, Frey et al 1990). Also, at the level of their local meta-theories, they have been used to develop another set of prescriptions $\mathbf{P}^{\text{DESC}}$ for the strategic entity A.

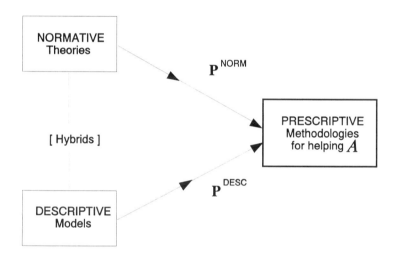

Figure 6.2   Prescriptions from theory-types

For strategic re-considerations in the sunk cost context, examples of each of the various types of prescription already exist. Taken together, however these currently present a somewhat confusing picture. Accordingly, in the following section, prescriptions derived from normative theory are re-structured around a concept of sunk cost *factors*. "Strategy as Rationality" is then proposed as a useful extension, involving the full set of the *backward-looking* rationalities.

Normative theory

The normative Principle of Ignoring Sunk Costs (*PISC*) states that: *Past expenditures by A, at a time* t_i *are "not relevant" to investment decisions by A at a later time* t_n, *where* $n > i$.

This is not to say that the past *per se* is irrelevant to prescriptive applications of $\mathbf{M}^{NORM}$. Far from it. The normative theory clearly recognises that past events and actions of *A* in earlier periods t_j, with $j < n$, are all quite relevant and important when specifying the parameters for any of the models in $\mathbf{M}^{NORM}$ and hence for the model-based prescriptions for $\mathcal{P}+$.

Specifically, past outlays by *A* on $\mathcal{P}-$ are recognised within the normative theory (or its local meta-theory) as partial causes of later events and conditions (e.g. reputation, motivation) in periods t_k, with $k > n$. Within the normative theory, these events and conditions, in turn, are then modelled as impacting upon the updated forecasts, the revised probabilities, the reset hurdle-rates, or whatever, that characterise $\mathcal{P}+$ and the alternative, [not $\mathcal{P}+$] with $\mathcal{P}^{ALT}$, exactly as depicted earlier (in chapter 5) with the generic *fake-casting* adaptation and interpretation of DCF use.

Several specific factors are recognised in $\mathbf{M}^{NORM}$ as comprising causal-linkages between *A*'s strategic behaviour, during $\mathcal{P}-$, and the subsequent evaluation of $\mathcal{P}+$. Such *sunk-cost-factors* may be separated out into direct and opportunity sunk-cost-factors, as follows:

Direct sunk-cost factors are events or conditions recognised as having been caused by *A*'s behaviour in $\mathcal{P}-$ and then affecting the evaluation of $\mathcal{P}+$ directly. These factors include *A*'s reputation (e.g. Weigelt et al, 1988), learning (e.g. Tang, 1988), information acquired (Majd et al, 1987), motivation (Leibenstein, 1976), and attained competitive position (Talmor, 1992).

Opportunity sunk-cost factors are recognised as having been caused by *A*'s behaviour in $\mathcal{P}-$ and then affecting the direct evaluation of [not $\mathcal{P}+$] & $\mathcal{P}^{ALT}$ the next best alternative to $\mathcal{P}+$. (i.e. affecting the opportunity costs and benefits of $\mathcal{P}+$). These include contractual obligations (Singer et al, 1987) and attained asset position (Pappas, 1976) which includes liquidity (in the case of *A* as a firm) and the myopic net-realizable-value (NRV). The latter is the estimated direct disposal value to *A* of the alternatively, the estimated net costs to *A* of a full clean-up of $\mathcal{P}-$.

Students and managers have often been berated for not ignoring sunk costs in the analysis of investment proposals. Yet, ironically, many of these "sunk cost factors" are often ignored in strategic analysis based

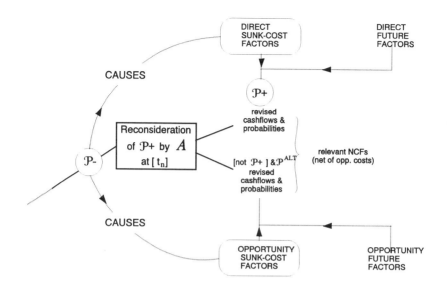

Figure 6.3 Sunk-cost-factors in the normative theory

upon the normative theory, when they should not be! In addition other future events and phenomena, not necessarily seen as causally linked to $\mathcal{P}$-, are also recognised within the normative theory $\mathbf{M}^{NORM}$ and its local meta-theory (discussed below) as affecting the forecasts, probabilities or hurdle rates, etc. associated with $\mathcal{P}$+. These factors may also be separated out into direct or opportunity subsets, as follows:

Direct future factors are arising in the future, without any recognised causal link to A's past behaviour, but impacting upon the direct evaluation of $\mathcal{P}$+. This class of factors delineates the scope and main focus of most strategic analysis in practice (e.g. Andrews, 1980). It includes such factors as forecast competitor and stakeholder actions (Singer et al, 1990), political or legislative factors (Porter, 1980), macroeconomic parameters (Haley et al, 1979), technological developments (Porter, 1980, Schwenk et al, 1991, Talmor et al, 1992), capital structure & systematic risk (e.g. Naylor et al, 1983), reversibility and future options associated with $\mathcal{P}$+ (Gupta & Rosenhead, 1968, Singer, 1987, Pindyck, 1991) and portfolio synergies (Karnani et al, 1985). A final class is comprised of:

Opportunity future factors i.e. factors arising in the future, without any recognised causal link to A's past behaviour, but recognised as affecting the direct evaluation of the alternative(s), [not $\mathcal{P}$+] & $\mathcal{P}^{ALT}$, etc. This includes the defensive NRV of the assets from $\mathcal{P}$- i.e. the Net Realizable Value after including such considerations as the potential impact on A of the buyer's future use of these assets (Schwenk et al, 1989). It also includes the Value of waiting, i.e. the special case where $\mathcal{P}^{ALT} = "\mathcal{P}+$ delayed" (McDonald et al, 1986).

In addition, normative theory has also offered alternative interpretations for a fifth distinctive class of factors, which is actually a strict subset of the above four classes. Factors in this class have each been considered within some m ϵ $\mathbf{M}^{NORM}$ as affecting the hurdle or discount rates for $\mathcal{P}+$. Examples of factors in this class are systematic risk, reversibility & future options, technological change and value of waiting.

Prescriptions and the meta-theories

As discussed in chapter four, the prospects are quite limited for extracting a useable set of prescriptive methodologies $\mathbf{P}^{NORM}$, from the normative (financial-economic) models, $\mathbf{M}^{NORM}$. These prospects are described in the "local meta-theory" developed by the creators of the normative models themselves. They are not optimistic. For example:

> "... our optimal investment rule critically depends on (various parameters)...but in fact it may be difficult or impossible to estimate them..." (Majd et al, 1987)

> "... parameters...may not be easy to measure." "..measuring these opportunity costs can be difficult" (Pindyck, 1991).

> "... one gets an apprehensive feeling about prescribing (rules for setting hurdle rates)." (Talmor et al, 1992)

> "I hope the theoretical treatment deepens economists understanding of the issue.." (Dixit, 1989)

The other more global meta-theories (i.e. meta-forecasting, meta-modelling, meta-rationality, mentioned earlier, in chapter 5) also endorse these *caveats*. In sum, convergent meta-theories are now telling us that attempts to prescribe strategy for A, using the forecast-dependent techniques derived from the normative models, i.e. $\mathbf{P}^{NORM}$, have not been particularly successful. The best that one can do, it appears, is to employ the generic fakecasting approach, using the normative theory simply to help identify generic issues or factors, including the various *sunk cost factors* identified above.

Descriptive models

Several other descriptive models of strategy with sunk cost, $\mathbf{M}^{DESC}$, have been shaped around empirical evidence, including evidence of the behavioural violations of the *PISC*. The various processes and prescriptions associated with the models $\mathbf{m} \in \mathbf{M}^{DESC}$ are set out in Table 6.1, below. These models combine elements of economic decision *content* (like forecasts) with specified cognitive &-or organisational *processes*, within $\mathbf{A}$.

Prescriptive interpretations of the models in $\mathbf{M}^{DESC}$, risk confusing *is* with *ought*; but the prescriptions ($\mathbf{P}^{DESC}$) associated with these models actually flow from several assumptions, embedded not in the formal theory itself, but in the local meta-theory. For example, if empirical evidence indicates systematic (and optimistic) biases in cashflow forecasts, or specific framing-effects in decision-making (e.g. $\mathbf{m}_1$, $\mathbf{m}_6$ in Table 6.1). Then it is argued in the local meta-theory that the strategic entity $\mathbf{A}$ *should* consciously attempt to counter such "bias" and "effects". Put differently the prescriptions from $\mathbf{M}^{DESC}$ mostly involve *meta-cognitive activity* within $\mathbf{A}$. Various existing prescriptions of this type are set out above in Table 6.1. These prescriptions may be further summarised, as follows:

1. *A should...*

(i)   Take into account various specified content factors in strategic re-considerations, particularly the sunk cost factors.

(ii)   Educate and train (subsystems) to counter the effect of cognitive bias, frames and mis-applied cognitive heuristics.

(iii)   Employ internal control tactics, including: setting prior limits (at t_0) on various measures associated with $\mathcal{P}$; Different decision-makers (for $\mathcal{P}$- and $\mathcal{P}$+); Tacit approval only (of $\mathcal{P}$-); improved reporting procedures.

2. *Researchers and-or A should...*

(i)   Re-think the traditional future-oriented planning framework.

(ii)   View strategic decisions within a "time stream" as distinct from a future-orientation.

Table 6.1
Descriptive models of strategy with sunk costs

Model m_i	Major Theme in m_i	Associated Prescription for A
m_i Staw (1980)	*Cognitive, Social:* Justification, norms of consistency, cognitive biases in judgemental forecasts	- set prior limits on outlays etc. - use different decision making subsystems, or tacit approval only - consciously compensate for systematic biases
m_2 White (1986)	*Cognitive:* Below-expectation performance triggers *framing* in the domain of losses for decisions at t_n. This causes risk-seeking behaviour, with a preference for options that make possible a return to the *status quo ante.*	- be aware of this effect of framing, in order to avoid exposure to the downside of risk-seeking. - predict or expect risk-seeking behaviour by others, following their below - expectation performance
m_3 Bowen 1987)	*General:* Information about strategy to date is often unreliable, ambiguous, equivocal	- be aware of that some situations lack hard decision criteria - be cautious about labelling decisions as "errors" *ex post* because "objective" assessment impossible *ex ante.*
m_4 Wernefelt & Karnani (1987)	*General:* qualitative, content-oriented	- be aware that past investments influence optimal strategic timing - be aware that past investments are footholds (i.e. attained market power) or windows (i.e. sources of information) that could increase the attractiveness of delay & flexibility. This effect is greater for larger firms.

m_5 Schwenk & Tang (1989)	*Cognitive, Social &* *content:* Interpretation of Economic factors mediated by cognitive processes of the strategic entity	- 	comply with m_1 (Staw, 1980) prescriptions be aware of learning curve cost reductions, forthcoming new technologies, non-myopic NRVs, i.e. defensive strategy
m_6 Bateman (1989)	*Cognitive & General:* Failure feedback triggers a frame for re-considerations. "Slack" prevents entity from following prescriptions of normative theory	- - -	compensate for framing effects consider influencing others by inducing frames conceptualize "time as a stream" in strategic decisions & re-considerations

Combining $\mathbf{P}^{NORM}$ (section 2 of this chapter) with $\mathbf{P}^{DESC}$ (section 3) now leaves A with the following three broader categories of model-based prescriptions (Figure 6.4) for guiding strategic re-considerations:

Category 1. *ENRICH the CONTENT:* Richly define the strategic alternatives (the formal objects-of-choice). Include consideration and analysis of the various *sunk cost factors*.

Category 2. *IMPROVE the PROCESS:* Implement the meta -cognitive, training & control processes, from $\mathbf{P}^{DESC}$, and....

Category 3. *DEVELOP NEW THEORY:* Search for alternative or complementary frameworks and paradigms from which to derive prescriptions for strategic re-considerations by A.

"Strategy as Rationality" is one development within the latter recommended category of "new theory" and frameworks.

Backward-looking-rationalities

The framework of "Strategy as Rationality" and the SCIO inquiry technique can be oriented to the context of strategic re-considerations with sunk costs (Figure 6.5) by focusing more closely on the backward-looking subset of the rationality-set $\mathbf{R}^{BAK} \subset \mathbf{R}$.

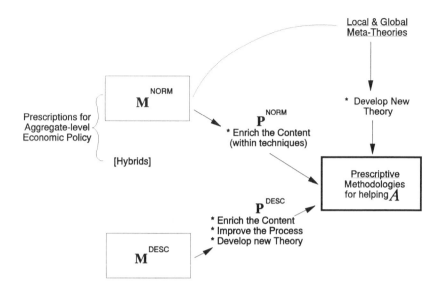

Figure 6.4   Generic prescriptions

The subset $\mathbf{R}^{\text{BAK}}$ contains all those forms of rationality that are defined with some direct reference to the past; the history of the agent A, or others. Specifically:

$\mathbf{R}^{\text{BAK}}$ = {*posterior, deliberative, selected, adaptive, open, natural, quasi, ratchet, retrospective, constrained, resolute, contextual,* etc.}

Some of these forms are foundations of more developed theories in Economics and Psychology. These include: *ratchet* (within Leibenstein's Economic theory), *selected* (within Nelson & Winter's Evolutionary theory), *quasi* (within Thaler's *Hybrid* theory), *retrospective* forms (within Staw's Psychological model). Each of these forms was briefly described earlier, in chapter three. The inquiry associated with each distinctive form of rationality is, inevitably, rather similar to the prescriptions for managers that have also been read into the corresponding developed aggregate-level theories. They are as follows:

RATCHET: A experiences inertia, takes into account cognitive costs of reconsideration and the benefits to A of co-ordination with others. etc. (Leibenstein, 1976).

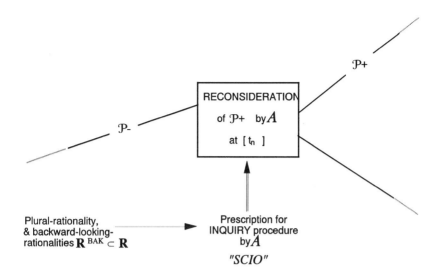

Figure 6.5 "SCIO" and backward-looking rationalities

Inquiry: (i) *What is the optimal timing and frequency of re-consideration? (ii) Does a choice of an alternative imply damage to A's reputation, violation of trust in A, or loss of A's co-ordination with others?*.

SELECTED: A adopts rules because of their survival value in the past. The past competitive environment is the source of behavioural rules for A (Marsh 1978, Hannan & Freeman 1977).

Inquiry: (i) *Will a habit and reputation of persistence (in similar situations) make A vulnerable to competitors with different strategies? (ii) Is there a risk to A of a war of attrition (in the market for $\mathcal{P}$+ outputs)?*

QUASI: A makes choices in accordance with Prospect Theory &-or Transaction-Utility-Theory. In either case, choices of majority of (or typical) entities depends upon their past behaviour (Kahneman et al, 1979, Thaler, 1985).

Inquiry: *What would the majority of A's decide if they were in this situation?*

RETROSPECTIVE: A assesses cost of violating the social norm of consistency, the benefit of being able to justify past decisions and actions of *A* (Staw, 1980).

Inquiry: *(i) If P+ is changed, abandoned, will A be perceived (by A or others) as inconsistent? (ii) Can a justification of P- be communicated. (iii) Have psychological biases (in forecasts for P+) been allowed for?*

A further subset $\mathbf{R}^{BAK*} \subset \mathbf{R}^{BAK}$ may also be identified. The various rationalities $\mathbf{r} \in \mathbf{R}^{BAK*}$ are not directly associated with any extant models or developed aggregate-level theories. They include *adaptive, posterior, deliberative, contextual, open, natural, constrained*, and *resolute* forms. Each of these is underdeveloped, in the sense that there is not yet any formal aggregate socio-economic theory based upon that form. Despite this, set $\mathbf{R}^{BAK*}$ now has the immediate potential to further extend prescriptions for meta-cognitive inquiry, at the level of the strategic entity *A*. *This step, in particular, represents one of the distinctive ways in which rationality can inform strategy* within the framework of Strategy-as-Rationality.

The various $\mathbf{r} \in \mathbf{R}^{BAK*}$ with their corresponding inquiries, are as follows:

ADAPTIVE: A incrementally updates past rules (March, 1978, Ansoff, 1991).

Inquiry: Does the experience with P- justify adjustments to A's policy guidelines, or other decision criteria.

POSTERIOR: A's goals are emergent, or interpretations of past actions by *A*. (Marsh, 1978).

Inquiry: What are A's goals now? Reformulate strategic goals in the light of P-.

DELIBERATIVE: A's goals are emergent, as learned capacities and potentials of *A*. (Rawls, 1972).

Inquiry: Does P+ utilise to the full A's newly-learned capabilities (competencies, capacities) developed during P-?

OPEN: A undertakes thorough or complete learning from past mistakes of *A* and others (Popper, 1989).

Inquiry: Have all mistakes in the history of P- been fully investigated and corrected?

NATURAL: Self criticism and self-correction enables *A*'s beliefs to converge towards a best representation of reality.

Has *A* been sufficiently critical of P- to date?

CONTEXTUAL: *A* should take actions oriented to maintaining institutions and traditions that express a "good life with others" (Habermas, 1984).

Inquiry: Is P+ part of a grand strategy P involving "the creation or maintenance of traditions or institutions that express A's vision of the good life with others"?

CONSTRAINED: It is not rational to abandon a *long-standing* personal plan for the sake of a newly-formed current preference (Slote, 1989).

Inquiry: (i) Is completion of P a long-standing unfulfilled mission of A? (ii) If P+ is changed, abandoned, will A be perceived (by others) as weak, and unreliable? (iii) Is continuation of P+ an opportunity for A to develop lasting habits (of task-completion) conferring future benefits?

RESOLUTE: *A* should sometimes adopt an overall plan that is expected to include a subsequent formally-dominated choice. *A*'s preferences will then subsequently be reshaped to respond to these already-adopted plans. Thus *A* should maximise "globally" over a life-span (McClennan, 1989).

Hence ask: If P+ considered in isolation fails on the updated criteria, was this situation foreseen in original evaluation of P? (ii) Is P+ part of a plan P that distribute benefits to A over an extended time?

If these questions based upon the *backward-looking* rationalities are attended to, the result is rather holistic and qualitative methodology, a variant of *SCIO*, for helping any strategic entity *A* to improve the conceptual model of strategy with sunk costs.

Meta-rationality

Finally, the various political and psychological conflicts surrounding strategic reconsiderations and especially the frequently misused principle of ignoring sunk costs (PISC), can now be cast into the framework of chapter 4, in which *meta*-rational arguments were used to forge a link between conflicting model-based prescriptions. Whereas models in $\mathbf{M}^{\text{NORM}}$, embrace *PISC* as part of their *meta*-theory, alternative techniques like *SCIO* do refer quite explicitly to the past activity of *A*. Like other model-based conflicts, this one can also be re-cast in terms of general *meta*-rational arguments involving the *backward-looking* rationalities, $\mathbf{r} \in \mathbf{R}^{\text{BAK}}$ and the *forward-looking* rationalities, particularly *RUM*.

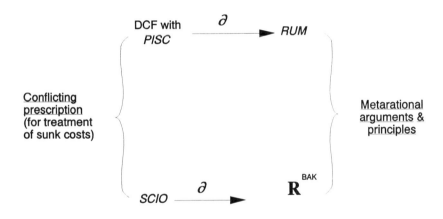

Figure 6.6. Sunk costs and meta-rational arguments

The various *meta*-rational arguments outlined in Table 6.2 below, then reveal the complex multi-dimensional nature of a balanced overall solution to the generic sunk cost problem. In the context of practical decisions involving sunk costs, where a strategic entity cannot be certain about preferences for the partially-defined and uncertain options $\mathcal{P}+$ versus [not $\mathcal{P}+$] & $\mathcal{P}^{\text{ALT}}$, a generalised appeal to alternative principles of rationality simply becomes a form of strategic wisdom, incorporating the themes set out in Table 6.2.

Table 6.2
Meta-rational arguments linking R^{BAK} with *RUM*

1. *ENRICHED DESCRIPTIONS:*

   For *RUM*, the description of Objects-Of-Choice must be "rich enough", possibly including factors causally linked to the past (exactly as depicted in terms of strategy in Figure 3, above).

2. *OPTIMALITY:*

   Within an economy-of-cognition, *A* should seek (i) *optimal rationality* i.e to balance non-forecastability against rule-worship. (ii) *optimal inertia* i.e. have triggered or timed re-considerations, or else some policy of non-reconsideration. (iii) *an evolutionary-optimum:* at some level of evolved intelligence, the benefits of additional intelligence are insufficient to justify the extra cost of sensory and nervous equipment, for **A**.

3. *CO-ORDINATION WITH OTHERS:*

   Inertia brings benefits of stability and clarity, increasing payoffs in many situations involving others. This works through *A*'s ability to enlist others, or to act as role model, because *A*'s intentions are always partly apparent to others.

4. *CO-ORDINATION WITH SELF:*

   Maximise lifetime-utility for *A*, a resolute (persistent) strategy generally enables development of more advanced capabilities and competencies. Therefore *A* should invest in a *generalised* capability for being resolute.

5. *EVOLUTIONARY STABILITY:*

   If every *A* (in a population or aggregate system) was a forward-looking utility-maximiser with respect to external rewards or prizes, then much time & effort would be *wasted* in long fights against others in a population for the "prizes" widely perceived as valuable. Such a *population* could be displaced by another that, for example, decides whether to fight by tossing a coin (Dawkins 1980).

6. *INSTITUTIONS:*

   Institutions are historically located and they also express or communicate values. Expressive actions cannot be reduced to *RUM* (e.g. Hargreaves-Heap 1989).

As indicated in the previous chapter, a similar argument about objects of choice also applies at the level of meta-theory, to the choice of theory with which to understand the strategy process, (e.g. Whittington 1993). Specifically, researchers in strategic management would be unwise to persist with old *paradigms* $\mathcal{P}^*$ that neglect some forms of rationality, just because they themselves have done so in the past (cf. Ansoff, 1991 *versus* Mintzberg, 1991). As indicated earlier, in chapter 5, re-considerations, adaptations and transitions are also called for at this higher level of strategic inquiry. In the following chapter, theories and paradigms of competition and *competitive* strategy are themselves reconsidered, from the perspective of Strategy as Rationality.

7. Competition

In the last decade or so, there has been an increasing awareness of the need to re-examine traditional paradigms dealing with economic competitiveness and business competition. The models and concepts of competitive strategy, as set out and popularised by Porter (1980 *et seq*) and others, undoubtedly remain quite useful, but they also appear unsatisfactory, incomplete or even contradictory, in many contemporary strategic management contexts. For example, recent studies of the level of competitiveness achieved by Asian firms (Schutte, 1994, Ritzer & LeMoyne, 1991) have contrasted their competitively successful strategies (and rationalities) of learning, co-operation and consensus, with the economic-rationality found in many Western firms, which emphasises measurement, control, efficiency and accountability.

This contrast become especially salient if one views "competitive" strategic entities not as traditional firms, or fortresses, but as knowledge systems and learning systems that co-evolve, learn and share information across boundaries and borders. It must again be asked "Which form(s) of rationality are correct?" (cf. chapter 3) Put differently, it may be asked "Which form of strategy is really more competitive?" This chapter answers that question, from the perspective of Strategy as Rationality. It offers a new and potentially rather constructive solution. First, however, it is necessary to discuss the concept of competitiveness and its uses in strategic management, in a little more detail.

In the dominant paradigm, the term "competitiveness" has been used in various ways, to mean:

(i)   The degree of cost-leadership of a firm, combined with the level of differentiation, or perceived quality, of its outputs (e.g.

Porter, 1980).

(ii)   The attractiveness of an industry as determined by the strength of the five "forces" in Oligopoly models, such as the threat of new entrants. (e.g. Porter, 1985).

(iii)   The combined strength, relative to a competitor, of several inter-related factors, e.g. production-capability; financial-capacity; marketing-effectiveness; political and economic environment, etc. (cf. Oral, 1986).

(iv)   The overall cost-structure and output capabilities of national economies (e.g. Porter, 1990).

Despite the fact that competitiveness is widely talked about, whilst its achievement has become a popular mission for corporations, nations and regions alike, the term "competitiveness" is itself rarely defined. When applied to nations, it usually means the same as productivity, or cost cutting, perhaps with some reference to economic infrastructure. When applied to corporations, however, it rarely carries any specific and coherent strategic implications (e.g. Oral, 1986, Oral et al 1989). Generally, "competitiveness" translates loosely as productivity and efficiency, an interpretation then put into practical effect as cost-reduction, process re-engineering, downsizing, re-sourcing and automation. Given current technologies, this leads in many cases to lower incomes for employees remaining within the boundaries of the more "competitive" strategic entity A, or increased numbers of unemployed, outside.

When many entities A_1, A_2,..., A_n do this, the result is social inequity and dislocations. Yet, paradoxically, missions of achieving international competitiveness have been held up as quasi-moral-imperatives, for management...all over the World. If every strategic entity is trying to achieve competitiveness in the usual sense, then how many can truly succeed? In this regard, Zeleny (1992b) recently noted that "The weak does not become stronger by freely competing with the strong: he is simply crushed". This is true for all "weak" entities, individuals, firms and nations, alike. Thus, the invisible hand of market competition becomes, for many entities, an very palpable iron fist.

Intertwined with the modern politics of competitiveness, there are at least two fundamental long-standing ambiguities in its conceptualization. Corporate managers and politicians alike must now confront these ambiguities as they attempt to formulate or advocate "competitive" strategies. The twin ambiguities concern:

(i)   The very nature, scope or boundary of the "competitive" strategic entity itself, i.e. Who or what is being "competitive" against *whom*? Put differently "Who is crushing, or bashing whom?" (cf. Krugman, 1994), and...

(ii)   The relationship between winning, or victory, *versus* success, or realisation-of-potential. This distinction and relationship, in turn, is evocative of the *plural* rationality of the strategic entity, with meta-rationality.

These two ambiguities are "twinned", or intimately related to each other, as "achieving competitiveness" could simply be taken to mean overcoming limitations within a singular strategic entity, A, such a nation-state, or industrial system, rather than necessarily outperforming or defeating multiple other entities $A_1, A_2, ..., A_n$. Thus the question of an entity's boundaries and the question of appropriate rationality concepts, with their competitiveness measures, must be discussed jointly and they must be co-determined. Accordingly, following a more detained discussion of these twinned ambiguities, a concept of competitiveness as the hyper-rationality of any strategic entity is set out, in this chapter. This new concept enables some resolution of the twin ambiguities, within the framework of strategy as rationality. Competitiveness as *hyper*-rationality (or, equivalently, *hyper*-strategy) is then made operational, as a new measure of the level of competitiveness of any entity, A.

Rationalities and competitiveness

Whilst the language and rhetoric of competitiveness can be exciting, it can too easily become a dangerous obsession, when used in inappropriate contexts (e.g. Krugman, 1994). Yet, ironically, it is rationality, not some dysfunctional "obsession", that lies at the heart of the economist's view of the world. This irony can be quite readily explained with reference to plural rationality together with relevant meta-rational criteria and arguments.

Many current theories and practical techniques of competitive strategy (e.g. Prescott et al, 1988) implicitly assume that managers are engaged in ruthless game-playing for their own interests directly, or indirectly on behalf of a firm. Put differently, economic entities are viewed as *rational utility maximisers (RUM)*. Competitive strategy is thus seen in terms of a barely contained conflict between warrior-like entities, an ingroup, the firm, or us... and an outgroup, the competition, or "them". These beliefs, when acted upon by many entities, or universalised, lead inevitably to a situation where: "Losers, and now even entire loser nations and states, are being...spawned...in abundance" (Zeleny, 1992b). The major alternative view sees a strategic-entity "competing" primarily against itself, or an imagined ideal version of itself, in a struggle to fully realise its own potential. Traditionally, concepts like "potential" and "capability" have belonged in the domain of psychology, not economics; but their importance to economic analysis has slowly become more widely recognised (e.g. Leibenstein, 1976, Tomer, 1987, Oral, 1986). The emphasis on "potential" in economics and strategic management is ultimately rooted in the idea that rational agents must not only have consistent preferences (*utility*) but they also have a duty to develop their own talents to the highest possible level...and to put them to good use. This idea appears in many of the strands that have at times been woven into the overall fabric of *plural* rationality, including *selective, systemic* and *expressive* forms, as well as ethical *utilitarianism*. With these elements of an expanded rationality-set in place, "competitive" strategy also becomes oriented towards developing capabilities within the strategic entity (e.g. Hayes, 1985) rather than simply outgunning rivals. These forms of rationality are much closer to meeting the evaluative *meta*-rational criteria, such as *universalisability* and *globality* (chapter 3). In addition, whilst they may not be *RUM*-captured, they can be made consistent with *RUM*, provided that the latter is placed within a *dynamic*, or evolutionary context (Axelrod, 1984, Singer 1988, Neilsen, 1989). In such contexts it is now well understood that the global success of any strategic entity A depends on the successful co-evolution of many other entities A_1, A_2,..., A_n, not on their defeat.

The competitive entity

Just as conceptions of rationality have become much more pluralistic, so too have forms of productive organisation, bringing with them attendant doubts about the traditional concepts of competitive strategy (e.g. Badaracco, 1991). In short, there is a nagging question of *whose* strategy and *whose* "competitive advantage" is being strategically managed. Who are "we" and *whom* are we playing against, *dis*-advantaging, "crushing" or "bashing"? To underline the seriousness of the problem, it is simply necessary to note that contemporary strategic managers and politicians have frequently expressed their concerns about achieving the competitiveness of...

(i)   **firms** ... in what is rapidly becoming a World of alliances, networks, flex-firms and multiple types of strategic-entity, many with permeable boundaries (e.g. Badaracco, 1991, Toffler, 1990, Moss-Kanter, 1991).

(ii)   **national** economies ... in what is fast becoming an inter-national or global economy (e.g. Porter, 1990, Moss-Kanter, 1991).

(iii) **traditional industries** ... in a what has already become a *post*-industrial society (e.g. Bell, 1973, Toffler, 1980, Zeleny, 1992) characterised by boundaryless productive entities, with convergent technologies and cultures.

As mentioned in the introduction to this book and in subsequent chapters, the possible candidates for the "competitive" strategic entity *A* in theories and models of competition could be selected from a rather long list, including:

Individuals or groups, a business segment or unit, a traditional firm or organisation, an alliance or coalition, an industry, a strategic-group, a set of players, a flex-firm, a hollow corporation, a network, a society, a nation, a region...

...or, conceivably, the entire productive human enterprise, viewed as a unitary whole (i.e. *"Metaman"*, cf. Stock, 1993). In addition to this long list of physical "competitive" entities, there are other, more abstract candidates for the players in abstract theories of competition, such as: living-systems, cognitive-systems and psychological-selves. Indeed, particular theories and models of strategy, competition and competitiveness have, at times, been applied to each of these types of entity. Yet the proper scope, in this respect, of many of the models and theories is almost always ambiguous and is often controversial, to say the least (e.g. Singer & Brodie, 1990).

For example, MIT Economist Paul Krugman has recently demonstrated that, insofar as one is concerned with the economic standards of living of the citizens of a large economic entity (e.g. USA, Japan or Europe) where most of the entity's outputs are consumed within that same entity, the concept of competitiveness should simply be taken to mean productivity. On the other hand, where corporations (e.g. Coke *vs* Pepsi) have become locked into a marketing war, so that one entity gains at the other's expense, competitive success takes on other meanings, such as relative market share.

This categorization (large nation-state *vs* traditional corporation) is by no means exhaustive. Smaller export-oriented national economies provide a third quite distinctive case, similar in many ways to large corporates. Unlike corporates, however, the political managers of small national entities remain quite directly concerned with the economic position of the entity's internal workforce, so to speak. Yet another, fourth distinctive case involves alliances and networks that are oriented towards co-operation, with the co-evolution of a set of entities (suppliers, customers and rivals, in Porter's terminology). Such strategies see corporate players, their employees and the competitor-set as co-evolving knowledge systems that come fully equipped with their own culture(s) or personality(s). As Richter (1994) has noted, if a *set* of competitors collectively fosters knowledge, they (or it) can more readily acquire the power to "dominate markets". Put differently, they develop a collective but still rather exclusive sustainability.

Hyper-strategy

Given these ambiguities, complexities and redundancies it now seems high time to ask seriously whether we can have one single all-embracing but nonetheless useful concept of "competitiveness". The meta-theoretic framework of Strategy-as-Rationality yields one such concept. The framework readily extends to yield a new concept of the *hyper*-**strategy** of any strategic entity, which may be operationalized as a generalized competitiveness measure. Hyper-strategy involves:

(i)   a **strategic entity** or agent A,

(ii)   the set **R** of the *plural*-**rationalities**, and

(iii)   **synergies** between distinctive forms of rationality.

The first two components have been elaborated throughout this book. The third component, synergy amongst multiple rationalities, has now emerged from recent studies of the competitiveness of industrial systems, by Ritzer and LeMoyne (1991). From a perspective of *Neo-Weberian* theory, these researchers were able to identify synergistic interactions amongst the four *Neo-Weberian* rationalities: *formal, theoretical, practical & substantive-value* forms, as these have co-existed within the Japanese industrial system, J. These synergies are the building blocks of their concept of the *hyper*-rationality of industrial systems. This concept could now be most usefully extended to embrace (i) the entire rationality set **R**, associated with (ii) the entire entity set **E**, or with a *plurally* rational strategic entity A.

"*Hyper*-strategy" provides a quite radical new conceptual model of competitiveness, that avoids many of the difficulties, mentioned above. It involves the subset $W \subset R$ whose elements are the four distinctive forms of rationality as defined in *Neo-Weberian* theory of industrial systems:

$$\mathbf{W} = \{\ formal,\ practical,\ theoretical,\ substantive\ \}$$

Each of these forms of rationality is defined below, where the terminology of "Strategy as Rationality" is then used to re-formulate and extend the Ritzer & LeMoyne analysis. The three structures within *hyper*-rationality are:

(i) $\mathbf{W} \sim \mathbf{S}$ correspondences (where **S** is the strategy-set).

(ii)   the associated *meta*-rational relations in **W** x **W**, and...

(iii)   the potential **synergies** amongst the $\mathbf{r} \in \mathbf{W}$.

Each is described in more detail in the remainder of the chapter.

(i)   W ~ S correspondences

The four rationalities $r \in W \subset R$ each correspond with some concepts (or sets of concepts) that are observed within Japanese industrial policy and strategy, as follows:

(a)   *Formal* ↔ *{ LRP, MITI }* Bureaucratic processes like formal Long-Range Planning, along with formal structures   like the Ministry of International Trade and Industry in   Japan are manifestations of Weberian *formal* rationality, i.e.   they are shaped around codified and generally applicable laws.

(b)   *Practical* ↔ *{ QCs, Brainstorming, Ringi }* The use of Quality Circles, Brainstorming, and "bottom-up" suggestions, in order to meet the challenges of improved   quality and new product development, are seen as examples   of Weberian practical rationality, i.e. they are expedient ways of pursuing a given practical end, in ways characteristic of "merchants and artisans".

(c)   *Theoretical* ↔ *{ Knowledge acquisition, R&D-focus }* Commitments to Research & Development and the acquisition of knowledge and information, together with general education in mathematics and economics etc. in the wider   society, are all seen as examples of Weberian *theoretical* rationality, i.e. mastery of reality by means of increasingly precise and abstract concepts, in ways characteristic of "intellectuals".

(d)   *Substantive (Weberian)* ↔ *{ systemic values }* Relative to individualism, the values of groupism, interpendence, harmony and obligation are seen as manifestations of Weberian *substantive* rationality, i.e.   where economic choices are guided by a consistent set of ultimate human values.

In the highly "competitive" Japanese industry, *J*, these four distinctive forms of rationality $r \in W$ are all observed to co-exist within the socio-economic system.   In contrast, American industrial systems are, according to Ritzer & LeMoyne (1991) predominantly *formally* rational, with the other forms absent, or only weakly manifest.   Moreover, *J* is observed to manifest synergies amongst the forms $r \in W$.

(ii)   *Meta*-rationality in *J*

Ritzer et al (1991) also noted the following examples of *meta*-rational relationships involving the *Neo-Weberian* forms, as they are manifested in modern Japanese industrial systems. These relations have the form $(r_i, r_j) \in W \times W$, as follows:

(*Theoretical, Practical*)   Abstract ideas help in the   attainment of practical ends.

(*Substantive, Practical*)   Practical living lays foundation   for spiritual activity.

(*Practical, Formal*)   Rules and laws are mindful of practical abilities and dispositions.

(*Theoretical, Substantive*)   There is an intellectual input to the (historical) development of (religious) value-systems, directly and *via* the political authorities.

(*Formal, Substantive*)   Particular "human" values exist within   a formal legal or economic system, e.g. welfare provisions.

(*Formal, Theoretical*)   Thereare scientific inputs to formal administrative procedures, like LRP, JIT, Statistical methods etc.

(iii)   Synergies in R x R

The concept of synergy is a very familiar one in the broad fields of strategy and systems.   In the strategic analysis of mergers and acquisitions, for example, it is quite common to make judgemental adjustments to model parameters in an attempt to capture expected "synergies", such as the cost savings and productivity gains that are beyond those that could be realised from mere co-existence of the separate entities. At a more abstract level, Beer (1972) has described the concept of a viable system as something more than the sum of its independently acting elements.   Now, with strategic entities more commonly being viewed as knowledge systems, it has become quite natural to think of synergy in terms of the productive integration of knowledge. Specifically, new knowledge might be created within an alliance by combining and integrating the knowledge embedded or sheltered within the separate entities. It is but a small step from this search for knowledge-synergies, to a more specific search for rationality-synergies, within a strategic entity.

Accordingly, the new concept of *Hyper*-rationality, as originally defined by Ritzer & Le Moyne (1991), refers to the synergy emerging from the co-existence of multiple rationalities. Weberian sociology and empirical observations of the Japanese industrial system (the entity *J*) have both shown that the rationalities could potentially reinforce one another. Thus the *hyper*-rationality of an industrial system is more than the mere co-existence of multiple forms of rationality within the entity, it is an emergent product of the entity's rationality-set. This idea of synergy may now be generalised (Figure 7.1) from **W** to **R** and from an "industrial system" to any strategic entity *A*, as follows:

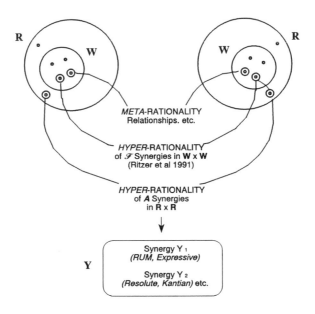

Figure 7.1 Synergy within plural-rationality

Define *v* as a mapping of *subsets* of **R** onto particular *synergies* or *hyper*-rationalities $y_i \in \mathbf{Y}$, i.e.

$$v \; : \; 2^R \Rightarrow \mathbf{Y}$$

$$v \; : \; \{r_1, \; r_2, \; r_j\} \Rightarrow \mathbf{y}_{i_1}$$

92

Then for any given strategic entity A we have:

$$\upsilon \ : \ 2^{R^{[A]}} \ \Rightarrow \ \mathbf{Y}^{[A]}$$

where $\mathbf{R}^{[A]}$ is the set of rationalities co-existing in A and

$$\mathbf{Y}^{[A]} \ = \ \{ \boldsymbol{y}_{i_1}^{[A]} , \boldsymbol{y}_{i_2}^{[A]} , \boldsymbol{y}_{i_{n[A]}}^{[A]} \}$$

where $\mathbf{Y}^{[A]}$ is the set of all the synergies realised in A amongst the set $\mathbf{R}^{[A]}$ and $n[A]$ = the number of distinctive synergies in A.

Ritzer et al (1990) offered some specific examples of synergies amongst *Neo Weberian* forms $\mathbf{r} \ \epsilon \ \mathbf{W} \subset \mathbf{R}$ that have emerged in Japanese industrial systems. Put differently, if J represents the Japanese industrial system as the strategic entity, the set $\mathbf{Y}^{[J]}$ contains the following elements:

$$\boldsymbol{y}_{i_1} \ = \ \upsilon \ (\{ \ theoretical, \ practical \ \})$$

An emphasis on knowledge increases the utilisation of lower-level skills in A.

$$\boldsymbol{y}_{i_2} \ = \ \upsilon \ (\{ \ practical, \ substantive \ \})$$

"Bottom-up" practical rationality is reinforced by the substantive rationality (ethic) of "groupism".

$$\boldsymbol{y}_{i_3} \ = \ \upsilon \ (\{ \ practical, \ formal \ \})$$

Bottom-up ideas improve the functioning of assembly lines and bureaucracies, e.g. Quality Circles.

$$\boldsymbol{y}_{i_4} \ = \ \upsilon \ (\{ \ Theoretical, \ substantive \ \})$$

Values of groupism and harmony (*wa*) strengthen the commitment of scientists, researchers etc. to contribute to the success of the enterprise.

$$\boldsymbol{y}_{i_5} = \boldsymbol{v}\ (\{\ formal,\ substantive\ \})$$

Values of groupism and harmony foster the development of the formally-rational permanent-employment system, which in turn reinforces the values.

To these examples involving *Neo Weberian* forms one must now add other potential synergies within a strategic entity, involving the *plural* rationalities r ϵ **R** as follows:

$$\boldsymbol{y}_{i_7} = \boldsymbol{v}\ (\{\ RUM,\ Expressive\ \})$$

Financial successes could be used to reinforce a sense of identity (e.g. IBM in the 60s)

$$\boldsymbol{y}_{i_8} = \boldsymbol{v}\ (\{\ Contextual,\ RUM\ \})$$

Financial success could be used to reinforce *A'* vision of the good life with others (e.g. BP supporting environmental groups)

$$\boldsymbol{y}_{i_9} = \boldsymbol{v}\ (\{\ Resolute,\ Kantian\ \})$$

A sense of duty and obligation could reinforce persistence with long-standing missions. (e.g. The United Nations Organisation)

$$\boldsymbol{y}_{i_1} = \boldsymbol{v}\ (\{\ Systemic,\ Expressive\ \})$$

Lessons from the past could be used to reinforce a sense of identity and autonomy (e.g. Federal Express learning from failure of the *Zapmail* project).

$$\boldsymbol{y}_{i_1} = \boldsymbol{v}\ (\{\ Strong\text{-}intensive,\ substantive\ \epsilon\ \mathbf{W}\ \}).$$

Formal models (e.g. market share models) may be used to reinforce the values of *A* (e.g. Market share forecasting in American Standard Corporation).

Thus, with the conceptual framework of "Strategy as Rationality" in place, implanting *hyper*-rationality (or equivalently, *hyper*-strategy) in any strategic entity A simply means (i) searching for ways of realising the synergies between elements of the rationality set $\mathbf{R}^{[A]}$ of *A*, and then (ii) identifying the absent synergies in $\mathbf{R}^{[A]} \times \mathbf{R}^{[A]}$, then taking appropriate steps to implant or to strengthen those synergies.

Operationalisation

There have been several previous attempts to measure the concepts of such as synergy and potential, in strategic analysis. As mentioned earlier, synergies is most commonly quantified as the judgemental adjustments to sales and financial forecast parameters, such as cashflows, earnings-per-share, market -share, etc. in the context of acquisitions planning. The concept of an organisation's "potential" was first measured in Beer's (1972) "Brain of the Firm" framework, but also, subsequently, in the PARE methodology of Derkenderen and Crum (chapter 5). More recently, the International Competitiveness Model (Oral, 1986, Oral et al, 1989) has been used to combine measures of a firm's actual and potential performance with measures of the macro-environments of the firm and its competitors.

 The new concept of *hyper*-strategy may now also now be translated into a quite general measure of the level-of-competitiveness of any strategic entity. The level of competitiveness of the entity *A* is simply the combined magnitude of the synergies in the set $\mathbf{Y}^{[A]}$, as follows:

$$\textit{level-of-competitiveness of } A = \sum_{r=1}^{n[A]} \mathrm{m}\,(y_{i_r}^{[A]})$$

where m (.) represents a measure of the synergies.

This new formulation of "competitiveness" of strategic-entities generalises across all types of strategic entity and all forms of rationality. Thus, it is itself universalisable and global. It emphasises constructive, positive changes in human systems, at all levels. Put differently, efforts directed at implanting hyper-strategy in order to increase levels of

95

competitiveness, thus defined, do not necessarily produce losers elsewhere in the system. Moreover, "achieving competitiveness", in this new sense, no longer means the same as seeking advantage...and *dis*-advantage, rather it becomes concerned with what is more broadly rational, right and good for all strategic entities within a larger human system.

Ultra-games

This new concept of competitiveness is a starting point for a generalisation and adaptation of traditional game theory, involving multiple strategic entities, of all types. In "*Ultra*-games", strategic interactions must be seen as occurring between any number of *plurally*-rational agents, A_1, A_2,.., A_r,... each of which operates in a multi-dimensional world of plural-goals, attentional limits, constrained autonomy and rational-ethical concern. Each entity A_i is engaged not in a search for utility maximisation, but in a search for competitiveness with reference to its own plural rationality dimensions and the associated synergies. Thus, each entity simply seeks partial satisfaction, or partial fulfilment...in a state of partial awareness; rather than the partial equilibrium of *Neo-classical* economics.

This conceptual model of an *Ultra*-game could prove quite useful in practice, without ever having to solve or even formulate an *Ultra* game in mathematical terms! Specifically, any strategic entity A_i could simply view other strategic entities as *plurally*-rational agents, with their respective hyper-strategies, rather than viewing them as rational *utility maximisers*, as in traditional game theory. Next, as a mere participant in an *Ultra*-game (rather than an observer or creator of the whole system) any given strategic entity A_i could simply attend systematically to the plural-rationalities of the other entities: A_1, A_2,..,A_r,..., with *their* opportunities for synergistic developments.

In this way, "Strategy as Rationality" can once again be made operational (cf. chapter 3) but this time as a "competitor" analysis technique, in which one entity systematically inquires into the "competitive" behaviour of other co-existing and co-evolving entities. Users of the adapted methodology simply need to retain a conceptual model of "other" entities as players in an *Ultra*-game. They only have to reflect upon a set of diagnostic questions that flow effortlessly from the *plural* rationalities, with synergies, as set out in Table 7.1. Thus, in practice, the players do not need any formal mathematical model of an *Ultra* game.

This new conceptual model of an *Ultra*-Game is nothing other than an adaptation of formal game theory models, comparable to the *fakecasting* adaptation of formal DCF (chapter 5). Like *fakecasting*, the adaptation of game-theory models provided by *ultra* games, with the diagnostics in Table 7.1, is intended simply to facilitate an ideological transition towards plural rationality, in the strategy process. In this regard, it is noteworthy that the more traditional and formal game theory, with its

Table 7.1
Directions for an intelligence effort

(a)   Competitor's beliefs (belief-rationalities)

1. *What are A_r's expectations about our moves?*
2. *Does A_r use extrapolatory forecasting?*
3. *Does A_r use conventional template planning?*
4. *Does A_r use sophisticate model-based forecasting system?*
5. *Does A_r conduct routine ex-post reviews of operations?*
6. *Are any of A_r's apparent beliefs (or statements) inconsistent?*
7. *Do A_r's recent actions indicate "blind-spots"?*

(b)   Competitor's calculations (means-rationalities)

8. *Does A_r have a record of actions based on non-obvious inferences?*
   (e.g. successful first moves)
9. *Is A_r using a model-based strategy-selection system?*
10.   *What are A_r's policy rules and established procedures?*
11.   *Is flexibility evident in A_r's strategic position?*
12.   *Has A_r postponed strategic moves, (i) to permit clarification of environmental trends   (ii) to correct internal deficiencies?*
13.   *Is there internal disagreement over goals or objectives?*
14.   *Does A_r use adaptive planning?*
15.   *What are implications of A_r's use of (a)   specific cognitive heuristics (e.g. availability, representiveness, anchoring) and (b) heuristic planning guides?*
16.   *What are A_r's capabilities?*
17.   *What is A_r's actual and potential level of performance?*
18.   *Does A_r use "pare" analysis. i.e. assessing potential, resilience?*
19.   *How strong is A_r's strategic momentum (status-quo preference)?*

(c)   Competitor's goals, motivations (ends rationalities)

20.   *What are A_r's stated goals or objectives?*
21.   *What goals are implicit in A_r's actions?*
22.   *Are these goals well-chosen, suitable?*
23.   *Can A_r's (a) current actual goals,   (b) strategic vision, be inferred from A_r's past behaviours, patterns, and statements?*
24.   *What is A_r's internal incentive structure?*
25.   *Does A_r balance shareholder value-creation against stakeholder interests in (i) actions, (ii) statements, and (iii) justifications?*
26.   *Does A_r have an ideological commitment, "hot spot", or mission?*
27.   *By what process or procedure does A_r formulate goals?*
28.   *How much importance does A_r appear to attach to this process of goal-formulation?*

(d)   Competencies: Practical, Expressive, Systemic Rationalities

29.   *Is A_r competent at implementation, "spiralling"?*
30.   *Does A_r have internal programmes of capability-development, in various functional areas?*
31.   *Is A_r skilled at matching capabilities to strategies?*
32.   *Does A_r have a corporate (or brand) (i) identity?   (ii) reputation? (iii) niche?*
33.   *Do A_r's past moves have symbolic value, reinforcing identity?*
34.   *Does A_r maintain traditions?*
35.   *How similar is the past and current context, for triggering the traditional responses?*

(e)   Competitor's ethical policies

36.   *Does A_r use (i) social cost-benefit analysis, (ii) utilitarian public justifications?*
37.   *Is there a record or policy emphasising fairness in the treatment of stakeholders?*
38.   *Does A_r recognise strategic duties and obligations?   How are these interpreted?*

(f)   Competitor Analysis and Interactive Rationality

39.   *Is there a pattern over time in A_r's actions or decisions?*
40.   *How does (analyst's) own situation affect the analysis of A_r?*

(g)   Synergies (*hyper*-strategies)

41.   *Does A_r apply its abstract knowledge to **increase** the utilisation of its own lower-level skills?*

42.   *Are A_r's routine practices fully **supported** by its expressed and cultivated values?*

43.   *Does A_r utilise experience at all levels of operation to continually re-design and **improve** its own procedures?*

44.   *Do the values and culture of A_r foster the advancement of scientific knowledge in ways that are **fully integrated** into A_r's systems and outputs?*

RUM rationality assumptions and its multiple solution concepts, has yielded very little in the way of practical methodology for strategic management (Singer and Brodie, 1990).

Conclusion

It is often said that modern managerial practices are several steps ahead of management theory. Successful managers are adapting their strategies to a rapidly changing environment, whilst abstract theories mature at a relatively slow pace. Therefore, to be useful, academics engaged in theory-building must sometimes look ahead and even jump ahead, in a spirit of pragmatic inquiry. They must also jump *sideways*, breaking free from the more traditional discipline-based approaches to understanding strategy. In so doing, they might be able to lift their own level of competitiveness, in the special new sense described here. It is this spirit that has led to the new concepts of competitiveness with their suggested operationalisations. For academics and managers alike, the local details of the new interpretation of competitive strategy are left deliberately sketchy, because they must be adapted by all thinking entities, in practice, to their own unique strategic situation.

8. Conclusion

This book began by noting that the role of rationality in strategic management has often been identified with the contribution from Economics. It was then asked whether or not other forms of rationality, conceived of and defined not only within Economics, but also in other branches of the social sciences, could also inform strategic management. At the same time it was noted that the concept of "strategic entity", the subject of theories of strategy, has also taken on multiple meanings. These have ranged from a psychological-self at one extreme, through firms, to a Global productive human system, at the other. The subsequent treatments of business ethics, model use, sunk costs and competition have demonstrated that the general theory of rationality does indeed inform and underpin an expanded theory of strategic management. For practicing managers, the fundamental implications of all of this, may be summed up as follows:

The things you should do as a strategic manager, acting on behalf of any of the types of strategic entity, are precisely the things you should do as an integrated and balanced person.

Thus, for example, all strategic entities should learn, develop capabilities and consider how their actions might evoke a response from others. In addition they should also have significant ambition or strategic-intent, be mindful of their future-selves and take into account the interests and needs of all other entities. All of these behavioral attributes are part of *plural* rationality, falling within the general theory.

The general theory of rationality (hence strategy) involves the beliefs, means and ends, or goals (cf. Tables 2.1-2.7). It also extends to meta-rationality and meta-ethics, that is:

(i)   meta-rational criteria for classifying the r ϵ **R**, (e.g. *belief-means-ends; aggregate-oriented, backward-looking*, etc.)

(ii)   evaluative meta-rational criteria for the r ϵ **R** (e.g. *global, universalizable, self-supporting*, etc.), and

(iii)   meta-rational & meta-ethical arguments, or relationships in **RxR** and their power-sets, that place the elements and subsets of **R** in relation to each other (e.g. *RUM-capture; beliefs-ends* relations, etc.).

As demonstrated throughout this book, much of the prescriptive theory of strategy now lies within this domain.

Meta-decision-analysis

For applications of strategy as rationality, various forms of *meta*-decision analysis (MDA) are needed. The SCIO technique (chapters 3) *fakecasting* (chapter 5) and *ultra-games* (chapter 7) may all be seen as elements of a more general MDA. The latter involves not only the choice of rationalities (SCIO) and the choice of models, but also the choice of language, or categories of meaning used in the strategy process.

Strategic decisions by all types of entity A have been variously characterised as *human, real-life, messes or conundrums*, that are *ill-structured, unprogrammed, wicked, intuitive*. However, despite the mess, there always remains a skeletal, or archetype decision structure. To even speak of a "decision" by an entity, there must indeed be some objects-of-choice, or strategic alternatives:

$$\mathcal{P}, \mathcal{P}^{ALT1}, \dots, \mathcal{P}^{ALTN}$$

...however vaguely and incompletely these may be perceived, articulated, or described.

In contrast with traditional managerial decision analysis, which involves a futile attempt to predict the cashflows and other consequences of each option, often over a planning horizon of several years (refer to chapter 5), MDA steps *backwards* into the domain of three inter-related *meta-*

decisions: (i) the decision about which of many forms of *rationality* to use, (ii) the decision about which (if any) *formal models* to use, (iii) the decision about which *descriptions*, or forms of language, to use, for describing, labelling and communicating the various strategic options.

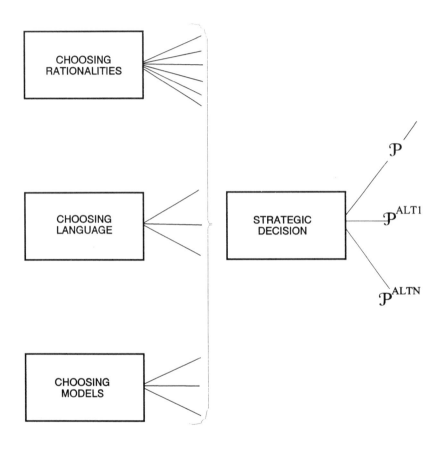

Figure 8.1 An archetype strategic-decision and its meta-decisions

In sum, for any strategic entity, and for any strategic decision with perceived alternatives $\mathcal{P}$, $\mathcal{P}^{ALT1},\ldots,\mathcal{P}^{ALTN}$ there are (at least) three *meta-decisions* (Figure 2) to be considered. The strategic entity A must...

(i)   *CHOOSE ITS RATIONALITIES* r ϵ **R** with reference to *meta*-rational criteria.

(ii)   *CHOOSE ITS FORMAL MODELS* m ϵ **M** with reference to *meta*-modelling criteria.

(iii) *CHOOSE ITS CATEGORIES* s ϵ **S** when generating multiple re-descriptions.

These three *meta*-decisions must be made in practice, by processes of reflection and discussion, as an expression of the free-will of the strategic managers who are acting on behalf of (any type of) strategic entity.

Decision errors

With this broader perspective on strategic decisions and their meta-decisions it becomes quite apparent that the concept of decision-error should no longer be confined simply to misapplied cognitive heuristics, nor merely *quasi*-rational behaviour, as has been the case in many earlier treatises on managerial decision analysis. The concept of "error" in strategic decisions must now be radically expanded, to include a much wider spectrum of choice at the *meta* level. Poor choices of rationalities, models and categories, or language, can most readily create confusion, despair, disparity and resentment in human systems. Thus MDA is but one device or tool intended to help overcome these rather important errors. Like *SCIO, fakecasting* and *ultragames*, the MDA approach could also act as a catalyst for transitions away from narrow strategic management ideologies.

Conflict management

Conflicts often arise in the strategy process, either at the meta-level (i.e. the left hand side of Figure 8.1) or at the level of the strategic decision itself (the right hand side). In the spirit of strategy as rationality, these must be managed through conversation and communication, within the entity *A*. Such conflicts can be managed by processes of resolution, settlement, or dissolution, as follows:

Resolution of decisional conflict within *A* involves re-descriptions of the alternatives $\mathcal{P}$, $\mathcal{P}^{ALT1}$,..., $\mathcal{P}^{ALTN}$ in such a way that a clear overall preference emerges within the entity (Schick, 1991). For example, a strategic divestment by a corporation could be described as "inevitably leading to the unwanted creation of a strong direct competitor", whereupon it is no longer considered desirable for the entity and the conflict is thus resolved.

Settlement: A decisional conflict within *A* could be settled, but not necessarily resolved, when an evoked description has compelling psychological force, causing the suppression (as distinct from counter-balancing) of other opposing considerations (Schick, 1991). In this case, latent conflict continues within *A* but it does not necessarily block rational action (Levi, 1986). For example, within Federal Express Corporation, in 1980, the notorious *Zapmail* project, requiring decisions about investment of hundreds of millions of dollars, was described in terms of "pioneering commercial applications of cutting-edge communications technology", a categorisation that effectively suppressed other known, opposing considerations.

Finally, a decisional conflict could be *dissolved* when the process of inquiry within *A* arrives at a configuration of redescriptions together with emergent preferences, that form a *Gestalt*, a sense of completeness, or harmony, or cognitive-equilibrium within the entity (Bourgine, 1989; Zeleny, 1989). The strategic problem is said to be dissolved, because its final formulation is its solution.

Language

In MDA the choice of cognitive categories, or language, for describing and perceiving strategic options is especially important. Every strategic entity *A* has to settle upon whatever descriptions and whatever language *it* thinks fit. This is indeed a most practical and pragmatic aspect of MDA. In the above examples, a divestment option that would have meant layoffs was re-described as inevitably leading to the creation of a strong direct competitor. Another investment was re-described as "pioneering the applications of communications technology", whilst the imperative of "paying down junk bond debt to improve the capital structure and reduce bankruptcy risk" might have been described as "felling one of the last remaining privately owned old growth Redwood stands" (cf. Poff, 1994).

According to Rorty (1985, p104), human beings can indeed change and improve themselves; they are capable of *remaking themselves*, he says, "by remaking their speech". MDA, with SCIO (chapter 3 & 7) and *fakecasting* (chapter 5) now invite or prescribe some rather similar processes of "re-making" of all types of strategic entity. With strategy as rationality in place, the revision and reconstruction of language and meanings has become has become a vital part of the production of an improved future self, or *autopoiesis*, for all strategic entities, not just individuals.

Conclusion

The various frameworks and methodologies set out in this book should prove immediately useful to any strategic entity that is grappling with the ambiguities and paradoxes associated with conventional strategic thinking. The associated prescriptions all take seriously the likely consequences of universal action based upon models, rationalities and language categories that are often quite dangerously narrow. The meta-theoretic framework of Strategy-as-Rationality, with its several extensions described throughout the book, are intended to reflect a wider spirit of *meliorism*: the belief that pragmatic improvement in the human condition is indeed possible.

Accordingly, the new framework and methodologies are all intended to direct the attention of all strategic entities towards the contemporary social, cultural and moral realities. In future, diverse permeable co-evolving strategic entities will re-make themselves, re-select their rationalities, revise their models and re-construct their categories. Put differently, they will engage in *strategic thinking without boundaries*, and to act accordingly. Perhaps one day these processes of thought and action will come to be seen as the proper mark of rationality, morality and competitive success; not only for individuals, but also for virtual-corporates and nation-states, alike.

Appendix 1

The main technical objections to **corporate rational-agency** have revolved around such considerations as informational and cognitive limitations, Arrow's social-choice theorem, General Systems Theory and the alternative political-process perspectives on strategy. However, reinterpretations of "rationality" have now emerged as a generic defence against all of these lines of attack, as follows:

(i) *Cognitive limits.* The neo-classical economic model has often been criticised for its implicit assumption of omniscience, or *perfect* rationality of the firm. Yet, in its description, Simon's concept of *bounded* rationality (an imperfect form involving *auto-*recognition of limitations) manifestly captures individuals **and** organisations as possible agents (e.g. Simon, 1987, Hogarth and Makridakis, 1981, Schwenk, 1984). This particular form of rationality has been interpreted almost *ab initio* as applying both to individuals, firms, or other cognitive systems. For example, both types of agent can be (and often have been) described as having attentional limits, some modest capacity for calculation and displaying satisficing behaviour that is mediated by the application of heuristic rules. Thus the organisation that is the subject of strategic management theory is at least a *boundedly* rational agent.

(ii) *Arrow's theorem.* Mainstream economic models of rational choice have upheld well-defined preference-orderings as the *sine qua non* of rationality. Arrow's (1963) theorem then proves mathematically that it is not possible to combine the preferences of several individuals into a single, well-defined collective preference structure. This is indeed an obstacle for advocates of collective agency. However, Levi (1988) has constructed an alternative theory of rational choice that does not rest upon preference-consistency. Quite the contrary, in fact: Levi's theory of rationality specifically accommodates unresolved value-conflicts within the agent. Thus, inconsistency of preferences, or value-conflict, has become a starting point for more realistic models of individual rationality, rather than the *coup de grace* for collective agency.

(iii) *General systems theory.* Re-defined rationality of another sort can be invoked to counter yet another line of attack on agency, rooted in General Systems Theory. According to Ackoff and Emery (1972) the existence of **purposeful subsystems** in organisations but not individuals undermines metaphors between the two. This argument can now be turned on its (metaphorical!) head. New theories of rationality (e.g., Elster, 1986) now hold that rational individuals **do** have autonomous psychological subsystems (i.e. "multiple selves"). Thus, in place of using the narrowly-rational individual as a metaphor for the firm, as in traditional economic theories, complex organisations are now being offered as metaphors for the individual, in psychological models. Once again, the *Hydra* returns, with another striking congruence between "rationality" and "strategy".

(iv) *The political process model.* Power and authority have traditionally been considered as alternatives to rationality, in explaining social phenomena. For example, Allison's (1971) political process model was proposed as an **alternative** to the neo-classical rational-actor model of the firm. Now, admitting politics into the mix no longer entails outright denial of rationality, as new forms of rationality proliferate. concepts such as forecasting and model-use (i.e. *intensive* or *strong* instrumental forms) and even the basic means-ends logic are now joined by younger forms having a distinctively political element. These include: *expressive, minimal, selective, deliberative* forms that have regard for political dimensions of behaviour such as identity and autonomy, information access, realisation of potential and fairness concerns. These forms are among the strands of the inter-woven fabric of *plural* rationality. Once again, it must be pointed out that very similar concepts are also integral to strategic management theory and research.

Appendix 2

The major *anti*-corporate-**moral**-agency arguments are quite vulnerable, as follows:

(i)   *MACHINE METAPHOR:* The organisation may be likened to a machine, controlled by **individuals** who must themselves accept moral responsibility (e.g. Danley, 1984).

This metaphor opposes CMA because it suggests that the individual managers are the only moral agents (i.e. blame drivers, not cars). However, the present identification of organisations as plurally rational agents, more akin to living systems than machines, completely undermines the metaphor, because such "machines" are not rational agents.

(ii)   *DESCRIPTIVE ETHICS:* Empirical social psychology and descriptive ethics sees groups and organisations as belonging to a different moral category from individuals. Group moral judgements are in fact distorted relative to the individual's conscience (e.g. Janis & Mann, 1977).

This is *anti*-CMA only if one argues from **is** to **ought**. To the extent that group decisions empirically fail to match individual's ethical standards, the need for linking strategy to ethics, with its implied concept of CMA, becomes that much greater.

(iii)   *CMA AS DIVERSION:* Arguments for CMA are harmful diversions from a moral crusade to the soul of individual managers (e.g. Rankin, 1987).

This *anti*-CMA argument does not make it clear whose attention is being diverted. In contrast, the new conceptual framework can be made operational as a technique for strategic analysis, that directs managerial attention to ethical concerns, alongside mainstream commercial issues (section 3, below).

The case for CMA may be further reinforced by an appeal to some independent *pro*-CMA arguments from business ethics and moral philosophy as follows:

(i)   *EMERGENCE:* this sees corporate conscience as an emergent property of complex, evolving, cognitive systems (e.g. Singer, 1984). Arguably, modern **corporations** are now at the critical stage of evolution where collective conscience is starting to emerge as a necessity of survival.

(ii)   *INTENTIONALITY:* This analytic argument (French, 1984) sees the internal decision structure of the corporation as the key to a meaningful description of **corporation** having the same moral standing as a hired individual who pulls the trigger.

In sum, denial of CMA has now become a barely tenable position. It could perhaps be sustained by insisting upon strictly *a*-rational foundations for ethics, like intuitionism or divine command theory.

References

Aaker, D.A., and Mascarenhas, B. (1984), 'The need for strategic flexibility' *The Journal of Business Strategy*, Vol. 5, No. 2, pp. 74-82.

Ackoff, R.L., and Emery, F.E. (1972), *On Purposeful Systems*, Tavistock.

Ackoff, R.L. (1983), 'An interactive view of rationality', *Journal of the Operational Research Society*, Vol. 34, No. 8, pp. 501-515.

Ackoff, R.L. (1979), 'The future of operational research is past', *Journal of the Operational Research Society*, 30, pp. 93-104.

Ackoff, R.L. (1981), 'The art and science of mess management', *Interfaces*, 11, pp. 20-26.

Allison, G. (1971), *The Essence of Decision*, Boston: Little, Brown.

Anderson, P., Arrow, K. and Pines, D. (eds.), (19xx), *The Economy as an Evolving Complex System*, Addison Wesley, Redwood City, CA.

Andrews, K.R. (1980), *The Concept of Corporate Strategy,* Irwin: Homewood IL.

Ang, J.S., Chua, J.H. and Sellers, R. (1979), 'Generating cashflow estimates: an actual study using the Delphi technique', *Financial Management*, Vol. 8, No. 1, pp. 64-67.

Ansoff, H.I. (1965), *Corporate Strategy*, New York: McGraw Hill.

Ansoff, H.I. (1987), 'The emerging paradigm of strategic behaviour', *Strategic Management Journal*, 8, pp. 505-515.

Ansoff, H.I. (1988), *The New Corporate Strategy*, Wiley: NY.

Ansoff, H.I. (1991), Critique of Henry Mintzberg's 'The design school: reconsidering the basic premises of strategic management', *Strategic Management Journal*, 12, pp. 449-461.

110

Argenti, J. (1980), *A Practical Approach to Corporate Planning*, Allen & Unwin, London.

Arrow, K. (1963), *Social Choice and Individual Values*, (2nd ed.), NY: Wiley

Arrow, K.J. and Hahn, F.H. (1971), *General Competitive Analysis*. North Holland: Amsterdam.

Axelrod, R. (1984), *The Evolution of Cooperation*, Basic Books, NY.

Badaracco, J.L. (1991), *The Knowledge Link: How Firms Compete Through Strategic Alliances*, Boston, HBS Press.

Bateman, T.S. and Zeithaml, C.P. (1989), 'The psychological context of strategic decisions: a model and convergent experimental findings', *Strategic Management Journal*, 10, pp. 59-74.

Baumol, W.J. (1987), 'The chaos phenomenon: a nightmare for forecasters', *London School of Economics Quarterly*, 1, pp. 99-114.

Baumol, W.J. (1989), 'Chaos: significance, mechanism and economic applications', *Journal of Economic Perspectives*, Vol. 3, No. 1, Winter, pp. 77-109.

Beach, L.R., Mitchell, T.R., Deaton, M. and Prothero, J. (1978), 'Information relevance, content and source credibility in the revision of opinions', *Organisational Behaviour and Human Performance*, 21, pp. 1-16.

Beer, S. (1972), *The Brain of the Firm*, Allen Lane: Penguin Press.

Bell, D. (1973), *The Coming of Post-Industrial Society: A Venture in Social Forecasting*, New York: Basic Books.

Bell, D.E., Raiffa H. and Tversky A. (eds.), (1988), *Decision Making: Descriptive, Normative & Prescriptive Interactions*, C.U.P. New York.

Bennett, P.G. and Huxham, C.S. (1982), 'Hypergames and what they do: a soft OR approach', *Journal of the Operational Research Society*, 3, pp. 41-50.

Bennett, P.G. (1985), 'On linking approaches to decision-aiding: issues and prospects', *Journal of the Operational Research Society*, Vol. 36, No. 8, pp. 695-669.

Bettis, R.A. (1983), 'Modern financial theory, corporate strategy and public policy: three conundrums', *Academy of Management Review*, 8, pp. 406-415.

Binmore, K. (1987), 'Modelling rational players', *Economics & Philosophy*, 3, pp. 179-214.

Bowman, E.H. (1980), 'A risk-return paradox for strategic management', *Sloan Management Review*, 21, pp. 17-31.

Bourgine, P. (1989), *Homo Oeconomicus is also Homo Cogitans. Theory & Decision* 27, pp. 1-6.

Bowen, M.G. (1987), 'The escalation phenomenon reconsidered: decision dilemmas or decision errors?', *Academy of Management Review*, Vol. 12, No. 1, pp. 52-66.

Bratman, M.E. (1987), *Intention, Plans and Practical Reason*, Harvard University Press, Cambridge, Mass.

Brock, W.A. (1991), 'Causality, chaos, explanation and prediction in economics and finance', In *Beyond Belief*, Casti, J.L. and Karlquist, A. (eds.), CRC Press.

Brunsson, N. (1982), 'The irrationality of action and action irrationaity: decisions ideologies and organisational actions', *Journal of Management Studies*, 19, pp. 29-44.

Bryman, A. (1984), 'Organisation studies and the concept of rationality', *Journal of Management Studies*, Vol. 21, No. 4, pp. 391-408.

Buchanan, A.E. (1985), *Ethics, Efficiency and the Market*, Rowman & Allenheld: NJ.

Bunn, D.W. and Salo, A.A. (1993), 'Forecasting with scenarios', *European Journal of Operational Research*, 68, pp. 291-303.

Burrell, G. (1989), 'The absent center: the neglect of philosophy in Anglo-American management theory', *Human Systems Management*, 8, pp. 307-311.

Camerer, C. (1985), 'Redirecting research in business policy and strategy', *Strategic Management Journal*, 6, pp. 1-15.

Cherniak, C. (1986), *Minimal Rationality*, Cambridge: MIT Press.

Cooke, V.J. (1985), 'The net present value of market share', *Journal of Marketing*, 49, pp. 49-63.

Cohen, L.J. (1981), 'Can human irrationality be experimentally demonstrated?', *The Behavioural & Brain Sciences* 4, pp. 317-370.

Colman, A. (1982), *Game Theory and Experimental Games, The Study of Strategic Interaction*, Pergamon: Oxford.

Cornell, B. and Shapiro, A.C. (1987), 'Corporate stakeholders and corporate finance', *Financial Management* (Spring), pp. 5-14.

Crum, R.L. and Derkinderen, F.G. (1986), 'Conceptual Development of Strategic Decision Models', In *Strategic Managament Research: A European Perspective*. (eds.), McGee, J. and Thomas, H., Wiley & Sons.

Cudd, A.E. (1993), 'Game theory and the history of ideas about rationality', *Economics and Philosophy*, 9, pp. 101-133.

Cyert, R.M. and March, J.G. (1963), *A Behavioral Theory of the Firm*, Englewood Cliffs, NJ: Prentice Hall.

112

Danley, J.R. (1984), 'Corporate moral agency: the case for anthropological bigotry', In Hoffman and Moore (eds.), *Business Ethics: Readings and Cases in Corporate Morality*, McGraw Hill, pp. 172-9.

Day, G.S. (1986), *Analysis for Strategic Marketing Decisions*, West Publishing Company: New York.

Davidson, D. (1980), *Essays on Actions and Events*, Oxford University Press, New York.

Dawkins, R. and Brockmann, H.J. (1980), 'Do digger wasps commit the Concorde fallacy?' *Animal Behaviour*, 28, pp. 892-6.

DeGeorge, R.T. (1990), *Business Ethics* (3rd edn.), New York: MacMillan.

De Geus, A.P. (1992), 'Modelling to predict or to learn?', *European Journal of Operational Research*, 59, pp. 1-5.

Derkenderen, F.G.J. and Crum, R. (1979), *Project Set Strategies*, Martinus Nijhoff, Boston.

Dewey, J. (1929), *The Quest for Certainty*, New York: Minton Balch.

Dixit, A. (1989), 'Entry and exit decisions under uncertainty', *Journal of Political Economy*, Vol. 97, No. 3, pp. 620-638.

Doktor, R.H. and Chandler, S.M. (1988), 'Limits of predictability in forecasting in the behavioral sciences', *International Journal of Forecasting*, 4, pp. 5-14.

Eden, C. (1989), 'Using Cognitive Mapping for Strategic Options Development and Analysis (SODA)', In Rosenhead, J. (ed.), *op. cit.*

Eden, C., Jones, S. and Sims, D. (1979), *Thinking in Organisations*, Macmillan, London.

Eerola, A. (1989), 'The role of general purpose forecasts in companies' strategic decision making', Presented at *Ninth ISF*, Vancouver.

Eilon, S. (1985), 'Structuring unstructured decisions', *OMEGA: International Journal of Management Science*, Vol. 13, No. 5, pp. 369-377.

Einhorn, H.J. and Hogarth, R.M. (1982), 'Prediction, diagnosis and causal thinking in forecasting', *Journal of Forecasting* 1982, 1, pp. 23-36.

Elster, J. (1979), *Ulysses and the Sirens*, CUP: Cambridge.

Elster, J. (1986), *The Multiple Self*, CUP: Cambridge.

Elster, J. (1986b), *Rational Choice,* Blackwell: Oxford.

Elster, J. (1989), *Solomnic Judgements: Studies in the Limitations of Rationality*, CUP: Cambridge.

Etzioni, A. (1986), 'The case for a multiple-utility conception', *Economics & Philosophy*, 2, pp. 159-183.

Etzioni, A. (1988), *The Moral Dimension: Towards a New Economics*, Free Press: NY

Feichtinger, G. and Kopel, M. (1993), 'Chaos in nonlinear dynamical systems exemplified by an R&D model', *European Journal of Operational Research*, 68, pp. 145-159.

Finlay, P.N. and Martin, C.J. (1989), 'The state of Decision Support Systems: A review', *OMEGA*, Vol. 17, No. 6, pp. 525-531.

Fischoff, B. and Goiten, B. (1984), 'The informal use of formal models', *Academy of Management Review* 1984, Vol. 9, No. 3, pp. 505-512.

Fishburn, P.C. (1991), 'Decision theory: the next 100 years?' *The Economic Journal*, Vol. 101, No. 404, pp. 27-32.

Freeman, R.E. (1984), *Strategic Management: A Stakeholder Approach*, Pitman, Boston.

Frey, B.S. and Eichenberger, R. (1989), 'Should social scientists care about choice anomolies?', *Rationality & Society*, Vol. 1, No. 1, pp. 101-122.

Friedman, M. (1970), 'The social resposibility of business is to increase its profits', *New York Times Magazine*, Sept. 13. 1970.

Friend, J.A. and Hickling, A. (1987), *Planning Under Pressure*, Pergamon, Oxford.

French, P. (1984), *Collective and Corporate Responsibility*, Columbia University Press: NY.

Fumerton, R.A. (1990), *Reason and Morality: A Defence of the Egocentric Perspective*, Cornell University Press: Ithaca.

Gardner, M. (1958), *Logic, Machines & Diagrams*, McGraw-Hill.

Garfinkel, H. (1967), *Studies in Ethnomethodology*, Prentice Hall: Englewood Cliffs, NJ.

Gauthier, D. (1986), *Morals by Agreement*, Oxford. OUP.

Gauthier, D. (1990), *Moral Dealing*, Cornell University Press.

Geanakoplos, J. and Pearce, D. (1989), 'Psychological games and sequential rationality', *Games and Economic Behavior* 1, pp. 60-79.

Gimpl, M. and Dakin, S. 'Management & magic', *California Management Review*, Vol. 27, No. 1, 1984, pp. 125-136.

Gladstein, D. and Quinn, J.B. (1985), 'Making decisions and producing action: the two faces of strategy', In *Organisational Strategy & Change*, J. Pennings & Assoc. Jossey Bass.

Glaser, R., Steckel, J.H. and Winer, R.S. (1992), Locally rational decision making: the distracting effect of information on managerial performance', *Management Science*, Vol. 38, No. 2, pp. 212-226.

Gleick, J. (1987), *Chaos: Making a New Science*, Viking, NY.

Goldman, A.H. (1980), 'Business ethics: profits, utilities and moral rights', *Philosophy & Public Affairs*, Vol. 9, No. 3, pp. 260-286.

Goodpaster, K. (1988), 'Ethical Frameworks for Management', In *Policies & Persons*, Mathews, J.B., Goodpaster, K. and Nash, L., McGraw Hill.

Grauer, M., Thompson, M. and Wierzbicki, A. (eds), (1984), *Plural Rationalities & Interactive Decision Processes*, (Springer-Verlag, Berlin).

Grinyer, P. (1992), 'A cognitive approach to facilitating group strategic decision-taking: analysis of practice and theoretical interpretation', *Knowledge and Policy: The Intl. J. of Knowledge Transfer and Utilization*, Vol. 5, No. 3, pp. 26-49.

Grubel, H.G. and Boland, L.A. (1986), 'On the efficient use of mathematics in economics', *Kyklos*, 39, pp. 419-442.

Gupta, S.V. and Rosenhead, J. (1968), 'Robustness in sequential investment decisions', *Management Science*, 15, pp. 18-29.

Habermas, J. (1981), *Theorie des Kommunikativen Handelns*, Frankfurt: Suhrkamprankfurt, McCarthy, T. (trans.), 'The Theory of Communicative Action', Boston: Beacon Press. 1984).

Haley, C. and Schall, L. (1979), *The Theory of Financial Decisions*, McGraw Hill.

Hambrick, D.C. and Mason, P. (1984), 'Upper echelons: the organization as a reflection of its top managers', *Academy of Management Review*, 9, pp. 195-206.

Hamlin, A.P. (1986), *Ethics, Economics and the State*, Wheatsheaf: Brighton.

Hannan, M. and Freeman, J. (1977), 'The population ecology of organizations', *American Journal Sociol.* Vol. 82, No. 4, pp. 929-964.

Hargreaves-heap, S. (1989), *Rationality in Economics*, Blackwell: Oxford.

Hayes, R.H. (1985), 'Strategic planning - Forward in reverse', *Harvard Business Review*, (Nov.-Dec.) pp. 111-119.

Henderson, B.D. (1983), 'The anatomy of competition', *Journal of Marketing*, 47, pp. 7-11.

Hiley, D.R. (1979), 'Relativism, dogmatism and rationality', *Int. Phil. Q.* 19, pp. 133-149.

Hirshleifer, J. (1976), *Price Theory and Application*, Prentice Hall: NJ.

Hitt, M.A. and Tyler, B.B. (1991), 'Strategic decision models: integrating different perspectives', *Strategic Management Journal*, 12, pp. 327-351.

Hogarth, R.M. and Makridakis, S. (1981), 'Forecasting and planning: an evaluation', *Management Science*, Vol. 27, No. 2, pp. 115-137.

Hollis, M. (1987), *The Cunning of Reason*, Cambridge: CUP.

Hosmer, LaRue T. (1991), *The Ethics of Management*, Irwin, Homewood IL.

Hunt, S.D. and Vitell, S.J. (1986), 'A general theory of marketing ethics', *Journal of Macromarketing*, Vol. 6, No. 1.

Jackson, M. (1990), 'Beyond a system of systems methodologies', *Journal of the Operational Research Society*, 41, pp. 657-668.

James, W. (1975), *Pragmatism* (Thayer, J.S. ed.) Harvard Univ. Press: Cambridge.

Janis, I.L. and Mann, L. (1977), *Decision Making: a Psychological Analysis of Conflict, Choice and Commitment*, NY: Free Press.

Jemison, D.B. (1981), 'The importance of an integrative approach to strategic management research', *Academy of Management Review*, 6, pp. 601-8.

Jungermann, H. (1983), 'The Two Camps on Rationality', In *Decision Making Under Uncertainty*, (ed.), by Scholtz, RW., pp. 63-86. Amsterdam: North Holland.

Jungermann, H. (1985), 'Inferential processes in the construction of scenarios', *Journal of Forecasting*, 4, pp. 321-327.

Kahneman, D. and Tversky, A. (1979), 'Prospect theory: an analysis of decision making under risk', *Econometrica*, Vol. 47, No. 2, pp. 263-291.

Kant, I. (1956), *Critique of Practical Reason* Beck, L.W. (trans.), Indianapolis: Bobbs-Merrill.

Karnani, A. and Wernefelt, B. (1985), 'Multiple point competition', *Strategic Management Journal*, 6, pp. 87-96.

Kavka, G. (1983), 'The Toxin Puzzle', *Analysis* , 43, pp. 33-36.

Kay, J. (1991), 'Economics and business', *The Economic Journal*, Vol. 101, No. 401, pp. 57-63.

Kervern, G.Y. (1990), 'Au Coeur des Strategies', In: *Entreprise la Vague Ethique*, Assas Editions: Paris. pp. 49-54.

Keys, P. (1988), 'A methodology for methodology choice', *Systems Research*, 5, pp. 65-76.

Kitchener, K.S. and Kitchener, R.F. (1981), 'The development of natural rationality. Can formal operations account for it?' *Contr. Hum. Dev.* 5, pp. 160-181.

Klammer, T.P. and Walker, M.C. (1984), 'The continuing increase in the use of sophisticated capital budgeting techniques', *California Management Review*, pp. 137-151.

Krugman, P. (1994), 'Competitiveness: a dangerous obsession', *Foreign Affairs*, Vol. 73, No. 4 (March-April) pp. 28-44.

Kuhn, J.W. (1992), 'Ethics in business: what managers practice that economists ignore', *Business Ethics Quarterly*, Vol. 2, No. 3, pp. 305-315.

Langer, E.J. (1975), 'The illusion of control', *J. Pers. Soc. Psych.* 2, pp. 951-5.

Langley, A. (1991), 'Formal analysis and strategic decision making', *OMEGA*, Vol. 19, No. 2, pp. 79-99.

Leibenstein, H. (1976), *Beyond Economic Man: A New Foundation for Microeconomics*. Harvard University Press: MA.

Levi, I. (1984), *Decisions and Revisions* CUP: Cambridge MA.

Levi, I. (1986), *Hard Choices: Decision Making Under Unresolved Conflict*, CUP: Cambridge, MA.

Linstone, H.A. (1984), *Multiple Perspectives for Decision Making*, Elsevier North Holland: New York.

McClennan, E.F. (1989), *Rationality and Dynamic Choice*, Cambridge: CUP.

McDonald, R. and Seigel, D.R. (1986), 'The value of waiting to invest', *Quart. J. Econ.* Vol. 101, No. 4, pp. 707-27.

Machina, M.J. (1989), 'Dynamic consistency and non-expected utility models of choice under uncertainty', *Journal of Economic Literature*, 27, pp. 1622-68.

MacIntyre, A. (1984), *After Virtue*, University of Notre Dame, Notre Dame, IND.

Mackie, J. (1978), 'The law of the jungle, moral alternatives and the principles of evolution', *Philosophy*, 53, pp. 455-64.

Mahoney, J.T. (1993), 'Strategic management and determinism: sustaining the conversation', *Journal of Management Studies*, 30:1, pp. 173-191.

Majd, S. and Pindyck, R. (1987), 'Time to build, option value and investment decisions', *Journal of Financial Economics*, 18, pp. 7-27.

Makridakis, S. (1988), 'Metaforecasting', *International Journal of Forecasting*, 4, pp. 467-491.

March, J.G. (1978), 'Bounded rationality, ambiguity and the engineering of choice', *Bell Journal of Economics*, 9, pp. 587-608.

Marsh, P., Barwise, P., Thomas, K. and Wensley, R. (1988), 'Managing Strategic Investment Decisions', In: *Strategic Management Research: A European Perspective*. (eds.) McGee, J. and Thomas, H. Wiley: Chichester, pp. 86-136.

Martinelli, A. and Smelser, N. (1991), 'A Sociological Perspective on Strategies of Dealing With Exogenous Complexity in Economic Analysis', In *Metatheorising in Sociology*, (ed.), Ritzer, G., Lexington Books: Mass. pp. 177-186.

Mason, R.O. and Mitroff, I.I. (1981), *Challenging Strategic Planning Assumptions*, Wiley Interscience.

McClennen, E. (1990), *Rationality and dynamic choice; foundational explorations*. CUP: Cambridge.

Mehrez, A. and Enrick, N.L. (1989), 'The meta-model of OR-MS', *OMEGA: International Journal of Management Science*, Vol. 17, No. 5, pp. 419-436.

Michael, D.M. (1989), 'Forecasting and planning in an incoherent context', *Technological Forecasting and Social Change*, 36, pp. 79-87.

Mill, J.S. (1962), *Utilitarianism (1861)*, Collins: London.

Mintzberg, H. (1977), 'Strategy formulation as an historical process', *International Study of Management & Organisation*, Vol. 7, No. 2, pp. 28-40.

Mintzberg, H. and Waters, J.A. (1985), Of strategies deliberate and emergent', *Strategic Managament Journal* 6: pp. 257-272.

Mintzberg, H. (1987), 'The strategy concept, 1 : five P's of strategy', *California Management Review*, Vol. 30, No. 1, pp. 11-24.

Mintzberg, H. (1990), 'The design school: reconsidering the basic premises of strategic management', *Strategic Management Journal*, 11, pp. 171-195.

Morecroft, J.D.W. (1983), 'Rationality and structure in behavioral models of business systems', *Proceedings of the 1983 International Systems Dynamics Conference*, M.I.T.

Morecroft, J.D.W. 'Executive knowledge, models and learning', *European Journal of Operational Research* 59, 1992, pp. 9-27.

Moss-Kanter, R. (1991), 'Transcending business boundaries: 12000 World managers view change', *Harvard Business Review*, May-June, pp. 151-164.

Myers, S.C. (1984), 'Finance theory and financial strategy', *Interfaces*, 14, pp. 126-137.

Myers, S.C. (1988), 'Note on an expert system for capital budgeting', *Financial Management*, Vol. 17, No. 3, pp. 23-31.

Munier, B.R. (ed.), (1988) *Risk, Decision and Rationality*. Reidel: Dortrecht.

Naylor, T.H. and Tapon, F. (1982), 'The capital asset pricing model: an evaluation of its potential as a strategic planning tool', *Management Science*, Vol. 28, No. 10, pp. 1166-73.

Nielsen, R.P. (1988), 'Cooperative strategy', *Strategic Management Journal*, 9, pp. 475-492.

Neitzsche, F. (1886), *Beyond Good and Evil*, Nauman: Leipzig.

Nelson, R.R. and Winter, S.G. (1982), *An Evolutionary Theory of Economic Change* Cambridge, MA. Belknap Press.

Nooteboom, B. (1989), 'Paradox, identity and change in management', *Human Systems Management*, 8, pp. 291-300.

Oral, M. (1986), 'An industrial competitiveness model', *IIE Transactions*, Vol. 18, No. 2, pp. 148-157.

Oral, M. (1987), 'A DSS design framework for competitive strategy formulation', *European Journal of Operational Research*, Vol. 28, No. 2, pp. 132-145.

Oral, M., Singer, A.E. and Kettani, O. (1989), 'The level of international competitiveness and its strategic implications', *International Journal of Research in Marketing*, 6, pp. 267-282.

Kral, M. and Kettani, O. (1993), 'The facets of the modelling and validation process in operations research', *European Journal of Operational Research*, 66, pp. 216-234.

O'Shaunessy, J. (1986), *Competitive Marketing: A Strategic Approach*, Boston: Allan & Unwin.

Osiel, M. (1984), 'The politics of professional ethics', *Social Policy*, Summer 1984, pp. 43-48.

Pappas, J.L. (1976), 'The role of abandonment value in capital asset management', *Engineering Economist*, 22, pp. 53-61.

Patterson, C.S. (1989), 'Investment decision criteria used by listed New Zealand Companies', *Accounting & Finance*, Vol. 29, No. 2, Nov. 1989.

Pennings, J.M. (1985), 'On the nature and theory of strategic decisions', In *Organisational Strategy & Change*, J. Pennings & Associates, Jossey-Bass.

Pierce, C. (1992), '*Reasoning and the Logic of Things*', The Cambridge lectures of 1898. Ketner, K.L. (ed.), Harvard University Press: Cambridge.

Pike, R.H. and Ho, S. (1991), 'Risk analysis in capital budgeting: barriers and benefits', *OMEGA: International Journal of Management Science*, Vol. 19, No. 4, pp. 235-245.

Pike, R.H. (1988), 'An empirical study of the adoption of sophisticated capital budgeting practices and decision-making effectiveness', *Accounting & Business Research*, Vol. 18, No. 72, pp. 341-351.

Pinches, G.E. (1982), 'Myopia, capital budgeting and decision making', *Financial Management*, Autumn 1982, pp. 6-17.

Pindyck, R.S. (1991), 'Irreversibility, uncertainty and investment', *Journal of Economic Literature*, 29, pp. 1110-1148.

Pinkwart, A. (1992), *Chaos und Unternehmenskrise*, Gabler Weisbaden.

Plott, C.R. (1982), 'Industrial Organisation theory and experimental economics', *Journal of Economic Literature*, 20, pp. 1485-1527.

Popper, K. (1989), 'The critical approach versus the mystique of leadership', *Human Systems Management*, 8, pp. 259-265.

Porter, M.E. (1980), *Competitive Strategy*, New York: The Free Press.

Porter, M.E. (1985), *Competitive Advantage*, Free Press. NY.

Porter, M.E. (1990), *The Competitive Advantage of Nations*, Macmillan Press, London.

Prescott, J.E. and Grant, J.H. (1988), 'A manager's guide for evaluating competitive analysis techniques', *Interfaces*, 18, pp. 10-22.

Prest, A.R. and Turvey, R. (1965), 'Cost benefit analysis: a survey. *Economic Journal*, 75, pp. 685-705.

Pruitt, S.W. and Gitman, L.J. (19xx), 'Capital budgeting forecast biases: evidence from the Fortune 500', *Financial Management*, Vol. 16, No. 1, pp. 46-51.

Pucik, V. and Hatvany, N. (1983), 'Management practices in Japan and their impact on business strategy', *Advances in Strategic Management*, 1, pp. 103-131.

Quinn, J.B. (1982), 'Logical incrementalism', *OMEGA International Journal of Management Science*.

Quinn, J.B. (1977), 'Strategic goals: process and politics', *Sloan Management Review*, Fall, pp. 21-37.

Radzicki, M.J. (1990), 'Institutional dynamics, deterministic chaos and self organising systems', *Journal of Economic Issues*, Vol. 24, No. 1, pp. 57-102.

Rand, A. (1964), *The Virtue of Selfishness*, Signet: NJ.

Rankin, N.L. (1987), 'Corporations as persons: objections to Goodpaster's "Principle of Moral Projection"', *Journal of Business Ethics* 6, pp. 633-637.

Ravetz, J.R. (1971), *Scientific Knowledge and its Social Problems*, Oxford: OUP.

Rawls, J. (1972), *A Theory of Justice*, Clarendon Press, Oxford.

Remus. W., O'Conner, M. and Griggs, K. (1993), 'Will reliable information improve the judgemental forecasting process?', Working paper. Dept. Decision Sciences, U. Hawaii.

Rescher, N. (1988), *Rationality: A philosophical Inqury into the Nature and Rationale of Reason*, Oxford: Clarendon Press.

Richter, F.J. (1994), 'Industrial organizations as knowledge systems', *Systems Practice*, Vol. 7, No. 2, pp. 205-216.

Rittel, H. and Webber, M. (1973), 'Dilemmas in the general theory of planning', *Policy Science* 4, pp. 155-69.

Ritzer, G. and LeMoyne, T. (1991), 'Hyperrationality: an extension of Weberian and *Neo*-Weberian theory', In *Metatheorising in Sociology*, Ritzer, G. Lexington Books: Mass. pp. 93-115.

Robinson, J.B. (1988), 'Unlearning and backcasting: rethinking some of the questions we ask about the future', *Technological forecasting and social change*, 33, pp. 325-338.

Rockart, J.F. and DeLong, D.W. (1988), *Executive Support Systems*, Dow Jones-Irwin, Homewood, Illinois.

Rosenhead J. (ed.), (1989), *Rational Analysis for a Problematic World* Wiley, Chichester.

Rossouw, G.J. (1994), 'Rational interaction for moral sensitivity: a postmodern approach to moral decision making in business', *Journal of Business Ethics*, Vol. 13, No. 1, pp. 11-20.

Rorty, R. (1982), *Consequences of Pragmatism*, Minneapolis: Univ. Minnesota Press.

Roy, B. (1993), 'Decision Science or Decision-Aid Science?', *European Journal of Operational Research* Vol. 66, No. 2, pp. 184-203.

Rumelt, R.P., Schendel, D. and Teece, D.J. (1991), 'Strategic Management and Economics', *Strategic Management Journal*, 12, (Winter 1991) pp. 5-29.

Russell, T. and Thaler, R. (1985), 'The relevance of quasi-rationality in competitive markets', *American Economic Review*, 75, pp. 1071-82.

Saloner, G. (1991), 'Modeling, game theory, and strategic management', *Strategic Management Journal*, 12, pp. 119-136.

Schendel, D. (1991), 'Editor's comments on the winter special issue', *Strategic Management Journal*, 12, (Winter 1991) pp. 1-3.

Schick, F. *Understanding Action: an Essay on Reasons*. Cambridge University Press, Cambridge, 1991.

Schoemaker, P.J.H. (1993), 'Strategic decisions in organisations', *Journal of Management Studies*, Vol. 30, No. 1, pp. 111-126.

Schutte, H. (1994), *The Global Competitiveness of the Asian Firm*, MacMillan.

Schwenk, C.R. (1988), *The Essence of Strategic Decision Making*, Lexington Books, Mass.

Schwenk, C.R. (1984), 'Cognitive simplification processes in strategic decision making', *Strategic Management Journal*, 5, pp. 111-128.

Schwenk, C.R. and Tang, M.J. (1989), 'Economic and psychological explanations for strategic persistence', *OMEGA: International Journal of Management Science*, Vol. 17, No. 6, 1989, pp. 559-570.

Sen, A.K. (1977), 'Rational fools: a critique of the behavioural foundations of economic theory', *Philosophy and Public Affairs*, 6, pp. 317-44.

Sen, A.K. (1987), *On Ethics and Economics*, Blackwell, Oxford.

Shank, J.K. and Govindarajan, V. (1988), 'Making strategy explicit in cost analysis: a case study', *Sloan Management Review*, Spring, pp. 19-29.

Simon, H.A. (1964), 'On the concept of organisational goal', *Administrative Science Quarterly*, Vol. 9, No. 1, pp. 1-22.

Simon, H.A. (1987), 'Rationality in Psychology and Economics', In *Rational Choice*, (ed.) by Hogarth, R.M. and Reder, M.W., University of Chicago Press, pp. 25-40.

Singer, A.E. (1994a) 'DCF without forecasts', *OMEGA: International Journal of Management Science*, Vol. 22, No. 3.

Singer, A.E. (1994b), 'Doing strategy as doing good: the new pragmatism', *New Zealand Strategic Management Journal*, 1, pp. 44-51.

Singer, A.E. (1994c), 'Strategic thinking without boundaries', Keynote address, In: *Proceedings of the International Conference on Interdisciplinary Research*, I.I.A.S. (Systems Analysis and Cybernetics). Carlsbad, Czech Republic, August 8-11, 1994.

Singer, A.E. (1994d), 'Strategy as moral philosophy', *Strategic Management Journal*, 15, pp. 191-213.

Singer, A.E. (1993a), 'Strategy with sunk costs', *Human Systems Management*, Vol. 12, No. 2, 1993b.

Singer, A.E. (1993b), 'Plural Rationality and Strategic Intelligence', In *Global Perspectives on Competitive Intelligence*, (ed.) by Prescott, J.E. and Gibbons, P.T. Published by the Society of Competitive Intelligence Professionals, Alexandra, Virginia. (August). pp. 351-366.

Singer, A.E. (1993c), 'Competitiveness as *hyper*-strategy', Paper presented at the Asia-Pacific Research in Organisational Studies colloquim, University of Hawaii at Manoa, December 1993.

Singer, A.E. (1992), 'Strategy as rationality', *Human Systems Management*, Vol. 11, No. 1, pp. 7-21.

Singer, A.E. (1991), 'Meta-rationality and strategy', *OMEGA: International Journal of Management Science*, Vol. 19, No. 2, pp. 101-110.

Singer, A.E. and Brodie, R. (1990), 'Forecasting competitor's actions: an evaluation of alternative ways of analysing business competition', *International Journal of Forecasting*, 6, pp. 75-88.

Singer, A.E. (1988), Book review of 'The Evolution of Cooperation' by Axelrod, R., *Journal of MacroMarketing*, Vol. 8, No. 1, pp. 59-61.

Singer, A.E. and van der Walt, N.T. (1987), 'Corporate conscience and foreign divestment decisions', *Journal of Business Ethics*, 6, pp. 543-552.

Singer, A.E. (1987), 'Measuring reversibility in capital budgeting', *Management Research News*, Vol. 10, No. 1, 1987, pp. 9-14.

Singer, A.E. (1986), 'The systematic enhancement of bottom-up financial appraisals', Presented to *TIMS-ORSA* 1986, Brisbane.

Singer, A.E. (1985), 'Stategic and financial decision making processes in New Zealand public companies', *New Zealand Journal of Business*, 7, pp. 33-46.

Singer, A.E., Davies, J. and Huang, M. (1984), 'Talking about probabilities: a logical problem for OR-MS', *Decision Sciences*, Vol. 15, No. 4, pp. 488-997.

Singer, A.E. (1984), 'Planning, consciousness and conscience', *Journal of Business Ethics*, 3, pp. 113-117.

Singer, A.E. (1981), 'Taking right-minded decisions', *Accountancy*, 92, 1058, pp. 114-7.

Slote, M. (1989), *Beyond Optimising*, Cambridge, Mass: Harvard U.P.

Smith, G.F. (1989), 'Defining managerial problems: a framework for prescriptive theorising', *Management Science*, Vol. 35, No. 8, pp. 963-981.

Staw, B.M. (1981), 'The escalation of commitment to a course of action', *Academy of Management Review*, Vol. 6, No. 4, pp. 577-87.

Stock, G. (1993), *Metaman*, Bantam Press: London.

Sugden, R. (1992), 'Rational choice: a survey of contributions from economics and philosophy', *Economic Journal*, Vol. 101, No. 407, pp. 751-785.

Sutherland, J.W. (1989), *Towards a Strategic Management and Decision Technology*, Theory & Decision Library. Kluver: Boston.

Tang, M. (1988), 'An economic perspective on escalating commitment', *Strategic Management Journal*, 9, pp. 79-92.

Talmor, E. and Thompson, H.E. (1992), 'Technology, dependent investments and discounting rules for corporate investment decisions', *Managerial and Decision Economics*, 13, pp. 101-9.

Teece, D.J. (1982), Towards an economic theory of the multiproduct firm', *Journal of Economic Behavior and Organisation*, 3, pp. 39-63.

Thaler, R. (1985), 'Mental accounting and consumer choice', *Marketing Science*, 4, pp. 199-214.

Thaler, R. and Sheffrin, H. (1981), 'An economic theory of self-control', *Journal of Political Economy*, 89, pp. 392-406.

Toffler, A. *Power Shift*, Bantam, 1990.

Toffler, A. *The Third Wave*, Bantam, 1980.

Tomer, J.F. (1987), *Organizational Capital : The Path to Higher Productivity and Well-being*, Praeger: N.Y.

Troye, S.V. (1990), 'Teorikriterier og Teorievaluering. Kompendium ved Norges Handelshoyskole', (Norway).

Tversky, A. and Kahneman, D. (1981), 'The framing of decisions and the psychology of choice', *Science*, 211, pp. 453-8.

Van Gigch, J.P. (1991), *System Design Modelling & Metamodelling*, Plenum: NY.

Van Peursen, C.A. (1989), 'Philosophy and Management', *Human Systems Management*, 8, pp. 267-272.

Wagner, H.M. (1988), 'Operations research: a global language for business strategy', *Operations Research*, Vol. 36, No. 5, pp. 797-803.

Walliser, B. (1989), 'Instrumental rationality and cognitive rationality', *Theory and Decision*, 27, pp. 7-36.

Weber, M. (1947), *The Theory of Social and Economic Organisation*, OUP: Oxford.

Weigelt, K. and Camerer, C. (1988), 'Reputation and corporate strategy: a review of recent theory and applications', *Strategic Management Journal*, 9, pp. 443-454.

Wensley, R. (1981), 'Strategic Marketing: Betas, boxes or basics?', *Journal of Marketing*, 45, pp. 173-182.

Werhane, P.H. (1983), 'Corporations, Collective Action, and Institutional Moral Agency', In *Corporate Governance and Institutionalizing Ethics* (eds.) Hoffman, W.M., Moore, J.M. and Fedo, D.A., Lexington Books: Mass. pp. 163-171.

Wernefelt, B. and Karnani, A. (1987), 'Competitive strategy under uncertainty', *Strategic Management Journal* 8, pp. 187-194.

White, G. (1986), 'Escalating commitment to a course of action: a reinterpretation', *Academy of Management Review*, Vol. 11, No. 2, pp. 311-321.

White, S.K. (1988), *The Recent Work of Jurgen Habermas: Reason, Justice & Modernity*, CUP: Cambridge.

Williams, B. (1985), *Ethics and the Limits of Philosophy*, Cambridge University Press.

Williamson, O.E. (1975), *Markets and Hierarchies: Analysis and Antitrust Implications*, Free Press: NY.

Wills, G. (1972), *Technological Forecasting*, Penguin Books: London.

Zeleny, M. (1992a), Editor's commentary on 'Strategy as Rationality', *Human Systems Management* Vol. 11, No. 1, 1992.

Zeleny, M. (1992b), 'Governments and free markets: comparative or strategic advantage?', *Human Systems Management* 11, pp. 173-6.

Zeleny, M. (1990), 'Why there is no theory of Perestroika', *Human Systems Management*.

Zeleny, M. (1990), 'Chaos and self organisation in companies', *Human Systems Management*, Vol. 9, No. 4, pp. 201-2.

Zeleny, M. (1989), 'Cognitive equilibrium: a new paradigm of decision making', *Human Systems Management*, Vol. 8, No. 3, pp. 185-8.

Zeleny, M. (1980), 'Strategic management within human systems management', *Human Systems Management*, 1, pp. 179-180.